mountain
bike guide

Derbyshire &
the Peak District

2009: 3rd Edition

Tom Windsor, Tim Banton &
Andy Spencer

ERNEST

www.ernest-press.co.uk

First published by The Ernest Press: 1991
Enlarged & updated edition: 1996
Reprinted with amendments: 2002
New & further enlarged edition: 2009

© Tom Windsor & Tim Banton.

ISBN 978 0 948153 89 1

British Library Cataloguing-in-Publication Data has been
registered with the British Library in Wetherby and is available
on request.

Typeset by Phil Hodgkiss Print & Design
Printed by Kyodo Printing Co

Disclaimer

Whilst we have made every effort to achieve accuracy in producing
the routes in this guidebook, the authors, publishers & copyright
owners can take no responsibility for trespass, irresponsible
riding, or loss or damage to persons or property suffered as a
result of the route descriptions in this guide.

Inclusion of a route in this guide does not guarantee that it will
remain a right of way. If conflict with a landowner occurs, please
be polite and leave by the shortest possible route – then check the
situation with the relevant authority. It is emphasised that riders
must give way to pedestrians and horse riders, and should make
every effort to warn others of their approach.

**Readers are reminded that mountain biking is an inherently
dangerous activity**

Introduction

The Routes

Route Details

Route	Miles	%age off-road	Time hours
1. Hayfield	16	81	4 1/2 hrs
2. Edale	14	79	4 1/2 hrs
3. Glossop	38	61	8 hrs
4. Ladybower	18	68	4 1/2 hrs
5. Stanage	23	52	5 hrs
6. Castleton	9	67	2 hrs
7. Bradwell	6	83	2 hrs
8. Buxton	15	60	3 hrs
9. Chelmorton	15	76	3 1/2 hrs
10. Baslow	22	55	4 hrs
11. Linacre	17.5	65	4 1/2 hrs
12. Chatsworth	19	74	3 1/2 hrs
13. Middleton by Youlgreave	15	80	3 hrs
14. Darley Bridge	18	45	3hrs
15. Ashover	7.5	60	1 1/2 hrs
16. Manifold	18	72	4 1/2 hrs
17. Derby North	25	40	5 hrs
18. Ashbourne	19.5	48	4 1/2 hrs
19. Doveridge	8	50	2 hrs
20. Ticknall / Robin Wood	9.5	48	4 1/2 hrs
21. Ticknall / Repton Shrubs	14	50	3 hrs
22. Gradbach	23	44	4 hrs
23. Minninglow	8	75	2 hrs
24. Bolsover	25	47	3 1/2 hrs
25. Locko Park	12	59	2 1/2 hrs
26. Bakewell & Monyash	26	46	4 1/2 hrs
27. Matlock & Carsington	36	51	6 hrs
28. Churnet Valley	28	40	4 hrs
29. Belper	12.5	52	2 1/2 hrs

Basemap of Cycle Routes

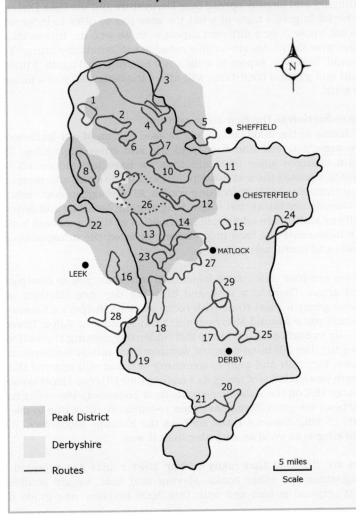

N

1
2
3
4
5
6
7
8
9
10
11
12
13
14
15
16
17
18
19
20
21
22
23
24
25
26
27
28
29

SHEFFIELD

CHESTERFIELD

MATLOCK

LEEK

DERBY

Peak District

Derbyshire

Routes

5 miles

Scale

Aims of this book

This book offers a range of circular off-road rides varying in length, difficulty and terrain, spread over Derbyshire and the Peak District. It hopes to give a taste of what the area has to offer to those who do not know it; or a different aspect to those who do. Unless stated otherwise the routes are largely rideable without dismounting. You should, however, expect to walk a few bits now and again. Fitness, skill and ground conditions will affect the distances you will need to walk.

Introduction to the new 2009 edition.

Welcome to the 2009 completely revised edition of our guidebook. We hope you will find it easy to use and enjoy the routes. The main changes since 2002 are that we have test ridden all the routes, updated the text descriptions and made small alterations or improvements to all 25 existing routes. All photographs are now in colour, as are the sketch maps. Height gain, facilities and nearest railway station are additional information at the top of each route. We have made the base map clearer, updated the information on trails and useful contacts.

There are four new routes which will introduce you to new paths and areas. There is a long and hilly big day ride (Matlock and Carsington), a short route with rocky sections (Belper), a limestone upland route around Monyash and a day route near Alton Towers, mostly in Staffordshire! I have test ridden our existing routes (from roughly Jan 06) in an array of weather from minus temperatures, snow, fog, rain and mud to scorching sun and still enjoyed them. There was evidence of heavy 4x4 use on some UC roads most notably Madge Hill on the Ashbourne route (now re-routed). Generally trail surfaces are good. Some have been re-surfaced; often due to use as part of long-distance trails such as the Pennine Bridleway. Way marking is as good as, or better than it was.

We are flattered that many of our 1991 routes are repeated in magazines and other books. Having said that, we are confident that original is best and with this 2009 revision, our guide has been made better still! We get positive feedback from many riders and a few grumbles at how tough some sections of the routes are. The difficulty of the routes obviously changes dramatically with the season and how wet, muddy and cold they are. We hope this guide remains a favourite of yours and provides many hours of pleasurable riding.

How to use this guide

The sketch maps are to be used with the route description as supplement not to replace an OS map. Use a large-scale 1:25 000 OS map when riding these routes. If you go off route they may prove vital!

Grid references are used to help locate starting points. If you are unsure how to use grid references see the margin of an OS Explorer map (eg White Peak) for an explanation. On the maps in this guide, the red arrow with DOT under it is a Direction Of Travel arrow and shows whether the route goes clockwise or anti-clockwise. The sketch maps in this book are not necessarily drawn to scale or of comparable scale to each other. We hope the instructions are easy to follow. If instructions do not say otherwise, continue on the track, path, road, line you are on, taking the most obvious well-defined route.

In many routes we mention gates, especially if they mark a change in direction, are a landmark, or at a junction. However do not assume we mention every gate. If, for instance, you are on a straight track with no possibility of getting lost, we may not mention that you have to pass through several gates as you ride along it (though usually we will). We use the term five-bar gate quite loosely to describe any wide, vehicle-width farm gate (it may have two, five or seven bars).

Remember
A: Only ride where you have a legal right to do so.
B: You cannot tell what a bridleway is like on the ground
       by merely looking at it on a map.

Writing your own routes

We hope you will enjoy our routes. Some of you will want to make changes, start and finish in different places, reverse the routes or make them longer and shorter. We expect some riders will want to make up their own routes. Here are a few pointers that may help with route planning:

» Think of a nice focus point or stop for food/break maybe a café or pub.

» Avoid main and busy roads.

» Look for added interest, woods, rivers, interesting buildings, good viewpoints, down hills!

» Tracks or bridleways that are walled both sides are often better surfaced in terms of being more rideable in wet weather although not necessarily smooth.

» Rougher bridleways are often easier to ride downhill than up.

» Steep climbs off-road can mean walking, on road they are often rideable.

» Look at the contours on your map carefully.

» Measure the distance of your proposed route and be realistic about your fitness, time or daylight available.

» Don't be too rigid about your rides, have a few options or amend them on the hoof (wheel) as you go along. An average mountain biker, not rushing might travel at about 7mph over the day including a few stops.

» Use the very good OS 1:25 000 scale Explorer maps.

» Get out there, explore and enjoy it!

Public transport to and within the Peak District

See the address section on pages 203-205 for contact details and information on train and bus services, including connection services.

REDUCING CAR USE

Lift share with friends so that you don't take 2 or 3 cars when you could take one.

If driving to a route, you can often easily start a route at the closest point to your home which may save 10 or 20 kilometres on your round trip.

Some routes are accessible by train. Where so, we have mentioned the nearest train station at the beginning of the route. Travelling by train with a bike is not always straightforward but if there are only 2 or 3 of you it is probably possible. The Derby to Matlock line will take bikes but it's a sprinter type with only room for two or three. Avoid very busy weekends. The Sheffield to Manchester line has lots of useful stations in the north of the peak, eg. Grindleford, Bamford, Hope and Edale.

Take a cloth or sponge with you so that you can give your bike a quick wash if it is really muddy before trying to catch the train home. Also carry a light set of clothes to change. Sometimes the Peak Park run a shuttle bus in the summer from Sheffield out to Stanage and Hathersage which will take bikes or climbing kit.

Derbyshire and the Peak District:
The Peak District National Park

In 1951 the Peak District was the first National Park to be established. By merit of its position, central within Britain surrounded by huge conurbations, it is very accessible (it is thought half the population of Britain is within 96km of Buxton) and consequently very heavily used by roughly 40 million visitors a year.

Its popularity could be considered one of its main problems, one with which planners continually wrestle. However do not let this put you off. Most people travel to the Peak in, and do not stray far from, their cars. On the whole they crowd particular tourist spots. You can still find solitude on many of these rides especially earlier or later in the day, midweek, off-season or in mixed weather. Usually on the off-road sections you will not see more than a handful of people on most routes: sometimes no one at all. Use public transport to, from and within the Peak Park/Derbyshire if you can.

LANDSCAPE AND ENVIRONMENT

Derbyshire and the Peak District offer plenty for the off-road enthusiast. It is an environment of huge variety; a landscape where lowland and upland Britain merge. The geology of the Peak Park can be considered in simple terms as a down-turned horseshoe-shaped section of gritstone in the north, curving down the east and west flanks, surrounding a more central area of shales and limestone.

The 'Dark Peak' area, with high moorland plateaux (peat, heather, bracken and grouse) and long dramatic gritstone edges, is juxtaposed with the very different shale and limestone features. Caves, cliffs, deep wooded dales, large quarries and lowland farms criss-crossed with mile upon mile of drystone walls are common features of the so called 'White Peak'. This landscape, shaped partly by climate and geology, has also been dramatically altered by man. Settlements, mill towns, factories, quarries and mines (for lead, fluorspar, coal, limestone and gritstone) as well as tourists have all made their mark and continue to do so. It is a complex but intriguing landscape, with the diversity and richness of several counties put together.

ACCESS AND ATTITUDE

People enjoy a wide range of outdoor pursuits in the Peak Park, which are not always completely compatible. User conflict can be a problem.

With walking as one of the most popular recreations, the Peak Park have in the past been cautious in their attitude towards mountain bikers but generally there are no problems and walkers and cyclists exist together happily in the Peak Park. Often a walker one day is a mountain biker on another!

The 'Open Access Land' marked on OS maps – some opened up by the recent CROW act – is private land on which there is a right to walk anywhere (except in grouse shooting season). However cyclists unfortunately have no such rights to ride on this land, except on specific rights of way such as bridleways. **Cycles have no right of way on footpaths. Please read the section on rights of way and take heed of the two codes of conduct below.** Be polite and give way to other users. Ride responsibly. Avoid badly churned ground where possible and try not to lock your wheels especially on descents. When following the routes in this guide please keep to the defined paths and travel at a quiet, unobtrusive pace. We suggest that groups should be no more than five or six riders. Horses are often frightened by or suspicious of bicycles. On approaching horse riders, slow to walking pace or stop and let them pass. If you want to pass ask the riders first if it is narrow and give them a wide berth.

OFF ROAD CODE
1   Keep to rights of way – use maps to plan your route in advance;
2   Check your bike before you set out;
3   Take adequate supplies of food and drink, waterproofs, tools and spares;
4   Give way to horses and walkers;
5   Ride in groups of two or three;
6   Be kind to plants and creatures;
7   Prevent erosion;
8   Close gates behind you;
9   Take your litter home and guard against fire.

THE COUNTRY CODE
1   Be safe – plan ahead and follow any signs;
2   Leave gates and property as you find them;
3   Protect plants and animals and take your litter home;
4   Keep dogs under close control;
5   Consider other people.
     www.countrysideaccess.gov.uk

Cycling and Conservation
Much of Derbyshire and the Peak District landscape has been shaped and changed by man; farming, industry, mining, quarrying

roads, building and tourism have all led to distinctive changes over hundreds of years and continue to do so. Increasing car use and visitor numbers, a high demand for all sorts of leisure activities and wider public access puts pressure on the countryside, and can lead to erosion problems or the loss of valuable habitats. While you are out pedalling you will notice how various organisations try to tackle heavy use or erosion problems. Laying huge gritstone flag stones from the floors of old mills (dropped in by helicopter) on wide boggy paths worn by walkers and cyclists on Howden Moor, the building of steps on Cut Gate or stone pitching and diagonal cut-off drains on Jacobs Ladder are three examples.

Mountain Bikes do cause erosion. Studies have shown that this is comparable to damage caused by walking boots. Heavy use in wet weather on soft, non-surfaced trails is often the greatest problem; delicate habitats and ground cover being easily damaged or entirely lost. Motorbikes and four-wheel drive vehicles with far more weight, power, size and very knobbly tyres cause many times more damage.

The landscape is and always will be changing but we can minimize the damage that we do as mountain bikers to the trails and the environment generally by considering where, when and perhaps more importantly how we ride. You could be more pro-active by using your bike to get around rather than your car and help by giving a practical hand. . . .

Practical conservation projects go on throughout the area both midweek and at weekends. There are many volunteer groups that you can help. I worked regularly for many years with a BTCV midweek group, but the Peak Park, DCC, National Trust and Derbyshire Wildlife Trust all run volunteer projects. You could help with conservation tasks that are directly linked to cycling such as drainage work on bridleways or hedge laying beside cycleways. Many other tasks such as tree planting, pond creation, footpath work or coppicing may not be linked to cycling, but do add to the rich landscape we ride in and enjoy. For contacts see the addresses section, page no 204.

Public right of way

To make the most of your off-road cycling you need to know where you can or cannot ride. In this section we hope to cover some of the basic terms you may come across to help you plan your own routes.

A **Public Right of Way** is a way over which all members of the public have a right to pass and repass.

PUBLIC FOOTPATH – over which there is right of way on foot only. Cyclists have no right of way to ride on a Public Footpath. Footpaths are sometimes waymarked on signs or marker posts by yellow arrows/discs.

BRIDLEWAY – over which there is a public right of way on foot, horseback and pedal cycle, provided that cyclists give way to horse riders and pedestrians. Bridleways are sometimes marked on signs by blue arrows/discs.

BYWAYS/BOATS – open to all traffic

RESTRICTED BYWAY – A highway for use only by walkers, horseriders, cyclists and horsedrawn vehicles but not cars or motorbikes – before 2006 classified as RUPPs. Restricted Byways may be marked by purple waymarks or arrows.

RUPPS – a road used as a public path. Its minimum status was that of a bridleway. However this classification proved unsatisfactory. All RUPPS should have been reclassified as one of the above, though old signs may still exist.

UNCLASSIFIED COUNTY ROAD – a minor road which may not be metalled. It can be regarded as having the same status as a byway. However they are not distinguished from any other road or private track on an OS map.

GREEN LANE – an unsurfaced walled track often of some antiquity. However the term Green Lane has no legal meaning.

TRAILS AND CYCLE TRACKS eg often converted old railway lines.

Canal towpaths

Many canals are owned or run by British Waterways and local

councils. There aren't any hard rules about which stretches you can ride. They may look ideal riding on the map but are not always as straightforward on the ground. For more specific details see addresses section page 204. (DCC or British Waterways).

Although every attempt has been made for routes to follow legal rights of way for cyclists, mistakes may have been made or changes in the network may have taken place. Since changes can and do occur, description of routes cannot be taken as proof of a path or track as being a right of way. So, if you are requested by a landowner who thinks you are trespassing, to leave the route you are on, please do not seek confrontation but be polite and leave quickly by the shortest practical route. If you believe you are in the right, check with the correct authority and ask them to deal with the problem. Don't give off-road cyclists a bad name.

Maps
To supplement the route descriptions or to plan your own rides use good large scale maps. The Ordnance Survey publish two 1:25 000 Explorer maps which cover most of the area in this guide: OL 24 - White Peak and OL1 - Dark Peak or use 1:50 000 Landranger Maps.

DEFINITIVE MAPS/HIGHWAYS MAPS (held by local authorities) Although public rights of way (footpaths, bridleways, RUPPS and byways) are shown on OS maps, changes may have taken place since they were printed. So if you are in doubt about the right of way, you should consult the definitive map for the area. Copies are held by county and sometimes by district and parish councils and some libraries. Unclassified roads are not recorded as such on OS or definitive maps unless they are also footpaths or bridleways ie they are not distinguished from tracks, drives or small roads. Since unclassified roads often provide ideal cycling it may be worth consulting the county highways map which records all highways maintainable at public expense. These are held by the local highway authority and are available for public inspection at county council offices. See addresses section page 204.

Equipment and Safety

A lot could be written here but too much advice might be confusing so briefly:

FIRST AID

Knowing some basic first-aid is always valuable, if not for yourself then for others. Courses run by organisations like the Red Cross or St. John's Ambulance are probably the best way to learn. A small first-aid kit might include; plasters, micropore tape, a selection of bandages, scissors and toilet paper.

PERSONAL IDENTIFICATION

If involved in a serious accident having some form of ID is useful. It helps to know if a person is asthmatic, diabetic, allergic to penicillin or has a rare blood group, as well as an address and next of kin contact.

» Tell someone where you are going and when you are likely to be back;

» Especially on longer rides try not to go alone. Two or three people is much safer and usually more enjoyable!

SAFETY ON THE HILL

Though Derbyshire and the Peak District are generally low level compared with other mountainous areas, we would advise reading the BMC's booklet on mountains. A lot of information in this may be relevant especially in winter on northern routes.

WEATHER

Be prepared for very changeable weather on the higher routes, especially the Edale, Glossop, Hayfield and Gradbach routes. The most useful weather forecasts are probably local ones such as daily forecasts displayed at the Peak Park information centres or available on line.

ALLOWING TIME

The times mentioned at the start of each route are only a rough guide, estimated by riders of medium fitness with average weather/ ground conditions. You will learn to judge your own riding speed or that of the slowest rider in your group. Always allow more time than seems necessary so a puncture or long dinner stop doesn't leave you caught out in the dark. Bad weather (especially rain, wind, snow and ice) or very wet/soft surfaces can double or triple the time you would normally take to ride an off road stretch. Leave more time for bigger groups.

CLOTHING – LAYERING UP

In summer often all you need are shorts and a tee shirt or short-sleeved cycle top. However maintaining a comfortable body temperature when mountain biking is sometimes difficult. Uphill you can get very hot and sweaty then on the downhills or on exposed ground quite cold. Most people find wearing a number of layers of the appropriate thickness works best. You can vary the layers, taking them on and off. Usually up to three layers (or more if needed) works well:

ONE: a short/long-sleeved base layer of wicking material (often synthetic but may be silk or wool) that will move moisture away from the body so there is a dry layer next to your skin.

TWO: a middle insulating layer that breathes well but traps warm air e.g. a synthetic fleece.

THREE: an outer layer of a windproof or waterproof jacket if needed.

Shorts/Trousers

For short journeys you can get away with normal shorts or trousers but on a longer ride or in wet weather specific cycle shorts with a pad and no uncomfortable seams are much better (lycra or baggies). Ron Hill nylon Tracksters or cycle tights are warm, dry quickly and don't flap about. In cold weather use thermal underwear.

Windproof/Waterproofs

Choose a breathable light-weight waterproof that packs down small, is cut for cycling with a longer back and arms and has reflective piping or patches. Some jackets have pit zips, holes under the arms to help ventilation. I prefer not to wear a waterproof unless it is very cold or raining reasonably hard. They do not breathe as well as a fleece or wind-shirt so can make you very sweaty and then cold.

Hands and Feet

Keeping hands and feet warm in winter when cycling can be a big problem. They don't move much and are very exposed to wind and water. Buy good gloves, a thin thermal 'buff' or similar (fits under your helmet) and carry them even if you don't think you are going to need them. Don't buy shoes or boots that are tight or wear too many socks as this will restrict the circulation making your feet colder. Some people like using waterproof socks, neoprene overshoes or winter boots. Others get on quite well wearing old leather walking boots. Cycling specific shoes have a stiff sole that doesn't flex too much. This makes pedalling more efficient and comfortable but make sure you can walk in them. Getting off the bike now and then will help warm feet up, as will making sure your body is warm enough so that it does not restrict blood flow to your extremities.

Helmets

It's good sense to wear a helmet when mountain biking. Modern helmets are light-weight, have adjustable bands to fit the head well and are well vented (i.e. cool) so they are comfortable to wear. Always try a helmet for fit before buying it. A peak can help keep sun or rain out of your eyes. Check a helmet has an EU standard (EN1078) or Snell B90/B95. Adjust the strap so the helmet sits squarely on your head protecting your forehead and is not easy to push back.

FOOD

When mountain biking you can consume a high number of calories and lose a lot of water through sweating. So, have a good breakfast before you set off. Eat something like a big bowl of oats or cereal for slow release carbohydrates. Always carry some snacks and sandwiches on longer rides, with sugars and carbohydrates that are easily broken down to replace energy. Drink plenty before and during your ride. You can lose litres of water per hour if it is very hot. Adequate fluid intake also helps prevent cramp. Tuck away some extra snacks for emergency rations.

MAP, COMPASS AND WHISTLE

Along with this guide book carry a large-scale map (detailed at the start of each route). Learn to use and carry a Silva-type compass (practise!). This could prove invaluable if you get off course. A whistle is useful for attracting attention and summoning help in emergencies. The international distress signal is six long blasts followed by a minute gap before repeating.

Your Bike

Since this guide was first written, mountain bikes have changed considerably. In 1991 most bikes had cro-mo steel frames, cantilever brakes, rigid forks, 7 speed gearing and flat bars. In 2008, mountain bikes are based around either a hard tail or full suspension frame made usually of aluminium and have disc brakes. They predominantly have a long travel fork, 9 speed gearing, wider handlebars and shorter stems. As riding styles have changed and technology advanced, the mountain bike has become more responsive to technical trails and forgiving on the rider. Bike weights vary depending on cost and inteded use.

CHOOSING A BIKE

Ideally you want a lightish bike that is strong, reliable and has good brakes. Low gear ratios are standard and tyres are readily available for all conditions - fat grippy tyres are best for the Peak District.

You don't need a very expensive bike to enjoy riding off road but a cheaper bike may be heavier and will have a lower specification of gears, wheels, brakes and other componentry. Before buying a bike, Ask advice from friends and your local bike shop. A full suspension bike needs careful set up and is more expensive to run as it will need constant maintenance to work reliably. The benefit is that full suspension is forgiving to the whole body and on a longer days riding, you will be less fatigued or 'beaten up'.

A hard tail bike usually weights less and can be more responsive. There is less maintenance required and if you are not riding on really rough or rocky terrain; a hardtail can be more than adequate. Suspension forks do take the 'buzz' out of a trail and are kinder on the wrists, neck and shoulders.

MAINTAINING YOUR BIKE
Get into the routine of washing and oiling your bike regularly. This prolongs the life of gear parts and the chain. By getting into a routine, your bike will become familiar to you. Regular cleaning can also solve problems before they develop; for example, a bent rear derailleur could cause your gears to skip indexing or worse still, allow your rear mechanism to go into the spokes.

You might see a small crack in the frame or fork or a cut/ split in a tyre. Also, you should check your chain regularly for stretch and replace it when required to avoid damaging the cassette and crank rings. You should also check your brake pads for 'life'. Have your bike serviced by a local bike shop or learn to do some of the maintenance jobs yourself.

The best way to wash your bike is immediately after a ride with warm water, a little bike cleaning solution and a brush or sponge. After cleaning, rinse the bike off, dry and re-oil the chain/cables. Derbyshire winter roads are heavily gritted and road salt is very corrosive on steel and alloy. If left on the bike, winter water with diluted road salt will cause havoc. Gears, brakes and cables can seize up. Alloy frames and magnesium forks can corrode badly.

TOOLS AND SPARES
A sensible tool kit would be: a pump, spare inner tubes, a puncture repair kit, tyre levers and a multi tool that includes all the Allen key sizes required for adjusting your bike. Most multi tools include a chain splitting tool and flat/star headed screwdrivers and a spoke key. On longer or more remote trips you might take zip ties, spare allen bolts, oil & a rag, spare spokes, duct tape, spare brake block/ pads and any specific tool that you bike may need, e.g. an air pump for your suspension.

VIBES FROM YOUR VELO

Learn to listen to your bike for creaks, rattles or squeaks, especially if thy are different from the usual ones. Feel for play in a loose headset or crank while riding and put it right before it becomes a major problem. Creaks are usually from a tiny amount of movement between aluminium/steel or two dry alloy parts. Copper grease on threads such as crank arms or bottom brackets can prevent creaking as water cannot get into greased threads. Noises can be from many places and sometimes not where you think they are coming from. A loose chain-ring, saddle or stem bolt can creak and should be tightened immediately. Similarly a loose quick release needs immediate attention. Full suspension bikes often suffer more creaks as the pivot points wear or become dry. Creaks are annoying but often not dangerous, however they can be a warning sign of something calamitous about to happen such as a cracked frame or fork, so don't ignore creaks rattles and squeaks!

Trails and Cycleways

Since our first edition of this guide in 1991, a lot of work has gone into promoting and improving cycle trails in the area, both by local councils and Sustrans. Many new trails have been opened as a result. There is good information on Derbyshire's trails on the internet and in leaflets. Derbyshire County Council produces a brilliant free leaflet with a map of all the cycle trails and lots of information and useful contact details. Below, I have listed the main trails but for a full list, pick up the above leaflet at a Tourist Information centre.

High Peak Trail

Map OS 1:25000 OL24 White Peak

The High Peak Trail is one of the longer trails in the Peak District, stretching 17½ miles from High Peak Junction on the Cromford Canal to Dowlow near Buxton. It follows the old Cromford Railway (closed in 1967) and joins the Tissington Trail just south of Parsley Hay. While scenic, varied and quite exposed; it is almost completely flat apart from three inclines: Hopton Incline is quite short but riding from Middleton to Middleton Top is steep and roughly 700m long. Ascending Sheep Pastures from the canal is a steady, steep ride and over a mile long. Cycle hire between April and October at Parsley Hay car park and also at Middleton Top Countryside Centre, Middleton-by-Wirksworth, DE4 4LS, Tel: 01629 823204.

Tissington Trail
Map OS 1:25000 OL24 White Peak
Together with the High Peak Trail, Tissington is the oldest of the Peak District trails (opened 1970) and runs for 13 miles from Ashbourne to Parsley Hay. Again it is almost flat, although there is a very slight slope down from the Parsley Hay on a good surface. The verges support a large number of wild flowers as do those of the High Peak Trail. Parsley Hay Cycle Hire Centre, Buxton. Tel: 01298 84493 and Ashbourne Cycle Hire Centre, Mapleton Lane, Ashbourne, Tel: 01335 343156.

Carsington Water
Map OS 1:25000 OL24 White Peak
There is a circular ride of about 8½ miles around the edge of the Severn Trent Water reservoir between Ashbourne and Wirksworth and is mostly offroad. The east side of the reservoir has quite a few gates but a good surface and is very scenic. It has a visitor centre, sailing club, fishing, cycle hire, watersports centre, café, shops and bird hides. Carsington Sports & Leisure, Ashbourne, DE6 1ST, Tel: 01629 540478 www.carsingtonwater.com.

Manifold Way
Map OS 1:25000 OL24 White Peak
Manifold Way follows the old light railway (1902-1934), the River Manifold for 6 miles through its scenic and heavily wooded valley and then the River Hamps for the final two miles. The smooth tarmac track curls between some interesting scenery. There is an old copper mine at Ecton and Thors Cave towers 250 feet above the valley floor. Wetton Mill has a good café. Cycle hire is available at the old station in Waterhouses. Manifold Track Old Station Car Park, Waterhouses, Staffordshire. ST10 3EG, Tel: 01538 308609 and at Brown End Farm Cycle Hire, Tel 01538 308313.

The Longdendale Trail

Map OS 1:25000 OL1 Dark Peak

An old railway track bed running beside Woodhead Reservoirs has been converted for use by walkers, cyclists and horses. It runs from the station at Hadfield to the entrance of the Woodhead tunnel, a distance of about 12 miles. See the Glossop Route that makes use of this trail.

Middlewood Way

Map OS 1:25000 OL1 Dark Peak

The track bed of the former Macclesfield, Bollington and Marple railway on the edge of the Peak District. 11 miles have been converted for recreational use between Macclesfield and Marple.

Trans Pennine Trail (TPT)

www.transpenninetrail.org.uk

The TPT is a mainly off-road, long-distance trail that runs coast to coast joining up the Irish and North Seas, from Southport or Liverpool in the west to Hornsea (NE of Hull) in the east. It is for walkers, cyclists and horse riders. The middle section crosses the Peak District north of Glossop and crosses the ridge of the Pennines.

Pennine Bridleway

www.nationaltrail.co.uk/PennineBridleway

A National Trail that is not finished at the time of printing. It currently runs from Middleton Top in Derbyshire to Yorkshire (near Settle) but will continue up to Northumberland. There are 130 miles open so far: 73 from Derbyshire to South Pennines, the 47 mile Mary Towneley Loop and 10 mile from Settle to Loop.

Opposite: Descent from Derwent Edge, Ladybower

1. Hayfield

Plainsteads Farm

1 mile

A624

Grouse Inn

N

D.O.T.

P Rowarth

Little Mill Inn

Lantern Rike

Glossop Road

Kinder Resr.

R.Sett

Sett Valley Trail

A6015

Birch Vale

Hayfield

P START

Chapel Road

Ollersett

Coldwell Clough

Hills Fm

A624

Route Details

Distance:

16 miles/26km

%age off road:

81%

Time:

4 hours

Height Gain:

760m

Map:

OS 1:25,000 Explorer
OL1 Dark Peak Area

Facilities:

Pubs, shops, cycle hire, toilets
and DCC info at Hayfield, and
other pubs on route.

Rail Access:

New Mills station only 2.5km
if you join the route at Birch
Vale (A6015).

Route Direction

Hayfield, Sett Valley Trail,
Peep-O-Day, Coldwell Clough,
Kinderlow End, Kinder
Reservoir, Middle Moor,
Plainsteads, Rowarth, Sett
Valley Trail, Hayfield Circle.

Route Summary

A compact route, strenuous
even for the fit rider but highly
rewarding for its fine views of
the west side of Kinder plateau
and the moorland areas that
surround Hayfield. Do not
forget to take your O.S. map
with you on this
ride; you will need it.

Start in Hayfield at the Sett Valley Trail carpark SK 036869. Follow the trail W for a good 1.2km, then turn L onto a small path (bridleway) next to a stile and large gate, opposite the end of the reservoir. On meeting the A6015, turn R towards New Mills, but after only 250 metres take the first road L. Climb steadily on tarmac for 1.6km, passing Birch Vale Quarries as you go. The tarmac deteriorates by Moor Lodge (buildings on the L). Continue uphill for about 500 metres ignoring the track which breaks off to the L (Piece Farm). Soon after the track levels, you should come to a junction. Laneside Road drops R. You should turn L on the bridleway.

You will soon go through a large gate, continuing uphill on the obvious track. The next 1.5km of bridleway follows this walled lane onto, then across the moors. In 1km from the start of this walled lane, having passed through two more large gates, you should come to a junction of paths. There will be a piece of open moorland (without walls) in front of you. Turn L on the bridleway just above the wall and follow this rather boggy stretch of track. After about 600 metres, just before Foxholes Clough, is a junction of paths (with a fingerpost). The bridleway L drops back into Hayfield. You should go straight on across the moor following the R-hand wall.

You will soon be riding along a walled lane again. Pass through several gateways and drop steeply to Hills Farm. Your bridleway goes through the farm's garden so please walk through quietly and shut the gate. Continue descending then ride along a flat but wet section, past Hills House to join the A624.

Go L but after only 100 metres turn R onto a track between a house and barn. It passes an old quarry then meets a large gravel track. Go almost straight across this track through the bridle gate signed Pennine Bridleway and follow the L-hand wall along the path to the second gate. Passing through drop diagonally L on the now surfaced, fast path with diagonal humps to a road. Turn R, ride downhill to cross the stream and go through a gate before

climbing up the road. Pass a farm at Coldwell Clough dated 1804
.

Shortly after this the surface becomes gravel. One track curves sharply R, a second goes straight on more steeply uphill. Take the latter. About 400 metres up this hill (some walking may be needed) you will come to a point where a path crosses yours and there is a wooden 4-way fingerpost. Continue straight on up to and through the next gate. There will be another gate immediately on your L. Ignore this but after a further 100 metres turn L by passing through a large gate onto moorland.

Have a look at your O.S. map now. You are now on the bridleway heading towards Kinder Reservoir. Follow the more or less flat path (a bridleway that is not very distinct on the ground) for about 150 metres and cross a sandy footpath. After a further 150 metres you will join a better path. Bear L onto this better path then follow it until you see a large wooden five-bar gate (the R-hand one) with stile and stone gateposts below Kinderlow End. Go through this gate, follow the bridleway as it bends L along a narrow walled section to a boundary post and large gate. Go L through this gate onto Hill House Estate.

To your R are good views of Kinder Downfall. Ride more or less straight on, on the obvious green path across a field to a small gate with stone posts. Continue down the next two fields and pass through a large gate onto a track beside the edge of the wood. Follow this stony farm track to a small road just below Kinder Reservoir.

Cross the road, go straight down the path, cross another service road then turn R to climb the steep zigzag bridleway onto Middle Moor. At first it is cobbled. At the first junction/corner (opposite the dam wall of the reservoir) turn acutely L and continue alongside the wall uphill. After a small open gateway bear L again. At the top, by a fingerpost and footpath, turn L. On meeting a track with a green metal sign go straight across. The white shooting cabin should be on your R. You will cross a boggy section on a new wooden bridge then ride between the heather on a fine sandy path. This path fords a stream, continues for roughly 800 metres then descends to ford a second stream before joining the A624 at Carr Meadow Farm.

Turn R uphill. After 800 metres take the first L signposted 'Charlesworth'. After about 1.2km take the first proper tarmac road L (marked dead end, and in a due W direction). Turn L again after only 100 metres (signed Pennine Bridleway, Lantern Pike, and Hayfield) opposite the footpath sign. An enjoyable, fairly flat tarmac stretch followed by a long descent will take you to a house and gate. Continue along an initially well-surfaced, walled track overhung by large beech trees to ford a small stream then climb uphill to a small road. Turn L and descend into Rowarth.

At the houses in Rowarth take the first L by Anderton House ('No Motor Vehicles Except For Access'). Pass a telephone box then go through the small gap between the fence and wall. Follow this narrow path, with a short bumpy section before you are on tarmac again. Curve L in front of the Little Mill Inn. Follow the road with a dead end sign for roughly 300 metres until a fork just before Laneside Farm. Ignoring the L, go straight on. You should now be on a rock-strewn track steeply uphill and initially more or less unrideable.

Pass a disused quarry to gain a flatter, sandy section of track before climbing again. Ignore a track L. Ride down the bumpy track past a farm with dogs (luckily most on leads) to join a road. Go L and 500 metres down the hill is a row of cottages on your L. Turn R on the bridleway opposite. On the first sharp bend L, go through the small bridleway straight on to descend the much narrower path. It is very bumpy but soon comes to a road. Turn L, then after about 200 metres L again through a bridle gate and onto the Sett Valley Trail. Follow the trail back to your starting point.

Opposite: Aidan and Dave, Heather Moors . Sometime dark clouds come to nothing. This day coninued to shine

2. Edale

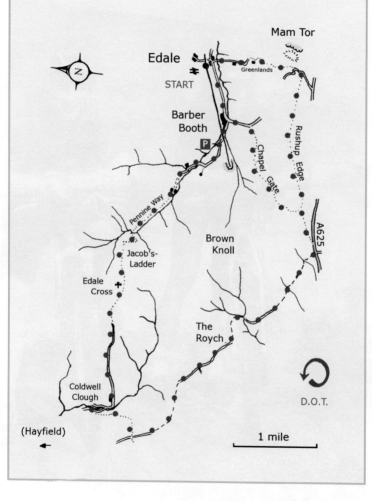

Mam Tor

Edale
START

Greenlands

Barber
Booth

Rushup Edge

Chapel Gate

A625

Pennine Way

Jacob's-
Ladder

Brown
Knoll

Edale
Cross

The
Roych

Coldwell
Clough

D.O.T.

(Hayfield)

1 mile

Route Details

Distance:

14 miles/22.5km

%age off road:

79%

Time:

4 1/2 hours

Height Gain:

Height Gain: 718m
(Rushup Edge option 768m)

Map:

OS 1:25 000 Explorer
OL1 Dark Peak Area

Facilities:

Cafes and pubs in Edale,
shop and pub in Hayfield
with a slight detour

Rail Access:

Station at Edale

Route direction

Edale, Barber Booth, Upper
Booth, Jacob's Ladder, Coldwell
Clough, Mount Famine, Roych
Clough, Chapel Gate or Rushup
Edge and Cold Side, Edale.

Route Summary

Edale is one of the few routes in
this book to be almost entirely
off road. It is a tough route
that uses some of the ancient
pack-horse routes that criss-
cross the Peak. The surfaces
are generally very rutted and
rocky. Most people would
need to do a fair amount of
walking on this route. It is
quite a high and exposed ride
with demanding terrain and
changeable weather so equip
yourself accordingly. Not
recommended for inexperienced
riders. This route would reverse
well but is still tough work!

Start at the carpark almost opposite Edale Station (trains from both Sheffield and Manchester stop here) SK 124853 or at the parking laybys between Barber and Upper Booth SK 107847. From the Edale carpark head R on the road towards Barber Booth. After nearly 1.2km you will cross the River Noe and then should turn immediately R to follow the road signposted 'Upper Booth'.

It passes under the railway and past the parking laybys mentioned earlier in the text. Roughly 800 metres of tarmac should bring you to a five-bar gate with a National Trust sign saying 'Lee Farm'. Go through the gate, up through Lee Farm, climbing gently to the bottom of Jacob's Ladder on a sandy, stony track.

On reaching Jacob's Ladder, ford the stream (or cross via the small but impressive packhorse bridge) before tackling the very steep zigzag path L. The bottom section is partially rideable, if you are very fit and good on rocky stuff. You will see the steps of the even steeper footpath to your R. Jacob's Ladder is very heavily used; as a route up to Kinder Scout generally, and to join the Pennine Way. The path is very rocky, steep and has suffered badly from erosion. However it has been stone pitched and the drainage has been improved. Some walking will no doubt be needed.

When at the top you meet a five-bar gate, you will probably want a rest, or have already have had about four. Push on through the gate on a short sandy stretch of badly rutted track till you reach the top of the hump. Go through an empty stone gateway. A medieval monument, Edale Cross, will be immediately on your R. The lump to your R is called Swine's Back.

There is now a very rough rocky descent which should be tackled with caution. About 1.5km will take you to another wooden gate. Pass through it still on a rough track, but over a grass field rather than moorland. Continue downhill past a fingerpost then onto a gravel track to a gate. Go through this and join the smooth tarmac road. Bliss! You are now at Coldwell Clough. The stream, a tributary of the River Sett, will be on your L. Pass a farm dated

1804 on your R and ride down to where the road forks and there are two gates. Pass through the L-hand gate.

Follow the road a short way uphill. Turn next L onto a way-marked bridleway climbing diagonally up the hill. Follow the obvious surfaced track (doubling back on the road slightly) on a stiff climb to a gate. Go through this gate then follow the wall and fenced bridleway to meet a larger track.

Turn L. Follow this rocky walled track for 400 metres, initially straight on and then as it curves L slightly. Continue until a number of gates and a sheepfold. Go through these and on uphill (open access sign). Follow the rutted resemblance of a track straight on, following the line of the R-hand wall. It is less than 800 metres to the next gate. The sandy, rutted track can be wet with large puddles. After the gate, if the weather allows, there is a good view of Chapel-en-le-Frith to your R.

You curve round below South Head and will be able to see Coldwell Clough to your L. Ignore the footpaths L and tackle the steep rocky section of track ahead that is banked on either side. What follows is 1km of rough descent. A short distance after the next gate a track joins yours from the R (a possible foul weather escape route?). Continue straight on to drop into Roych Clough.

At the bottom, ford two streams before climbing again. The next 800 metres have been stone pitched and is mainly rideable if dry (with a little grunting). Follow the gated sandy track. Cross the small stream at Bolehill Clough, curve R, pass Tom Moor Plantation and ride on to meet the A625 road from Chapel. Take the small concessionary bridleway L. This leads onto Rushup Edge gated UC Road/Bridleway.

You are now about an hour or less away from your starting point in Edale. Nearly 800 metres up this very badly eroded track with large rock steps (some walking) you come to a large gate followed by a cairn and signpost. On the other side of this gate are options A and B:

(Option A)

Turn L and follow the bridleway known as Chapel Gate that will shortly descend steeply. It curves R at first. Ignore a small path which forks L by a wooden post and continue to follow the more distinct track. Drop downhill with care on a very badly eroded path with huge ruts and narrow ribbons of tarmac to balance on. Pass through gates as necessary and continue until you meet a road. Turn L downhill to Barber Booth and then along to your starting point, at Edale or Upper Booth parking layby.

(Option B)

Go straight on up to and along Rushup Edge (splendid views in clear weather). At first the track follows just L of the wall. However after about 500 metres there should be a small wooden gate in this R-hand wall. Go through this gate, off the well-defined path which becomes a footpath, onto a poorly defined bridleway, and almost immediately through a large gate.

This goes along parallel to the wall on moorland but on the R-hand (S) side. If you come to stiles and locked gates you have obviously missed the small gate and need to backtrack to find it. On the correct path you should reach a metal five-bar gate. Go through this and drop downhill to a smaller wooden gate then meet the road. At the road turn L and cycle just over the brow. From here either follow the road steeply downhill to Barber Booth or turn R on the bridleway (a small gate shortly after the highest point of the road, i.e. almost immediately). In fact two bridleways run from this gate.

Take the L-hand one which descends to Hardenclough Farm and then Edale. Again it is sandy and eroded by water but all rideable and really good fun. It will bring you out on the road between Barber Booth and Edale, very close to your starting point.

Opposite: The author climbing Jacob's Ladder. The famously challenging climb that mountain bikers pit themselves against

3. Glossop

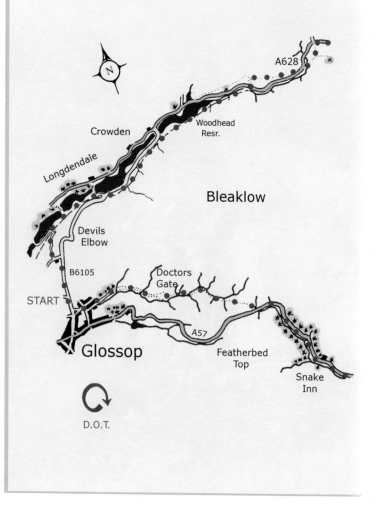

N

A628

Crowden

Woodhead
Resr.

Longdendale

Bleaklow

Devils
Elbow

B6105

Doctors
Gate

START

Glossop

A57

Featherbed
Top

Snake
Inn

D.O.T.

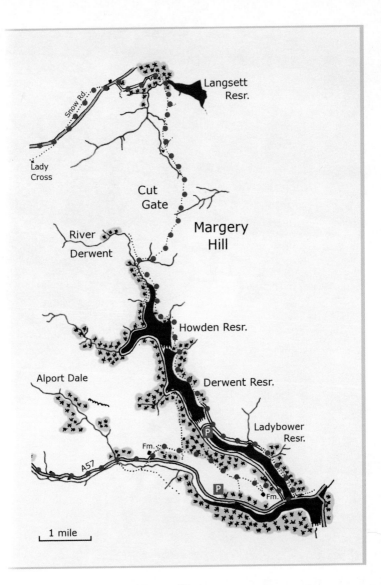

John and Ryan, Roych Clough, Edale Route

Route Details

Distance:
38 miles/61km

%age off road:
61%

Time:
8 hours (Yes honestly)

Height Gain:
1040m

Map:
OS 1:25 000 Explorer
OL1 Dark Peak Area

Facilities:
Pubs and shops at Glossop,
tea kiosk and cycle hire near
Derwent Dam at Fairholmes
car park (SK 172893) Pub
near Langsett (SE 178011)

Rail Access:
Nearest station Bamford
5.5km if you start the route
at Ladybower Reservoir
(Ashopton Viaduct near
Crookhill Farm)

Route direction

Glossop, Woodhead Reservoir,
Longside Edge, Lady Shaw,
Snow Road, Milton Lodge,
Swinden Lane, Mickleden Edge,
Cut Gate, Ladybower Reservoir,
Bridge-End Pasture, Snake
Road, Doctor's Gate, Glossop.

Route Summary

Glossop Circle is the longest
and probably toughest route
in this book. It is, however,
very rewarding with a real
variety of terrain and views,
and a high moorland feel.
Its height, length and rough
ground conditions mean it is
vital to go properly equipped
and allow lots of time. It took
us about 8 hours in dry, fine
conditions. It begins with road
and straightforward hard-
packed track then tends to get
rougher as you progress. The
route involves some difficult
'technical' sections.

Start in Glossop on the B9105 (Woodhead Road), which passes the railway staion, SK 035942. (A good alternative start point would be the Heatherdene Car Park, near Ladybower Reservoir SK 202680.) The ride starts by climbing out of Glossop in a northerly direction. Pass Cemetery Road on your left (signposted Padfield) then 1.2km further on choose the next L, Padfield Main Road.

Turn R immediately after passing between two small reservoirs. A pleasant downhill with sharp corners drops you to a bridge over the Longdendale Trail (now signposted Trans Pennine Trail). Only 200 metres past this look for the waymarked bridlegate and path on your R onto the trail. Turn L and follow the trail for an easy 3km to cross the B6105 and then a further 6.5km on the flat to the blocked Woodhead Tunnel. At the tunnel turn R up the gravel track for 100 metres then go sharp L opposite the carpark layby onto a steep path signed TPT East. Cross the A road and pass through the bridlegate signed TPT Dunford Bridge. Struggle up this steep path to join another track on Pikenaze Moor. Turn R signed TPT again.

The track has a good cinder/stone surface which stays dry in most conditions. After passing through another gateway the track climbs and dips, traversing Longside Edge before joining the road again roughly 4km from where you left it.

Cross the road with care and go through the small gap in the crash barriers opposite. Drop down the track to cross Salter's Brook by a narrow stone bridge before climbing straight on, alongside Ladyshaw Dike. Where the track curves L follow it N across the moor to meet the A628 opposite a road junction.

Turn R and follow the road for 1.7km. At the top of the hill you should be able to see a triangulation point on your L. Ignore the two bridlegates on your L but shortly after this go L on the marked byway next to a road sign warning motorists of sheep. It leaves the road at an acute angle to pass through a wooden five-bar gate. This 'Snow Road' is a grassy track through a mass of young heather and bilberry plants. It is rutted, just 1.8km in length and all downhill until you re-meet the road. There is a pub here which may prove very welcome for food or drink.

Turn L onto the road but after about 500 metres go R down a waymarked track (bridleway) beside a house. Go through a metal five-bar gate and descend for roughly 200 metres. Look out for a fingerpost L. Go to and through a large gate. If you pass this, go L at the sharp R-hand corner which will bring you to the same gate at Swinden Lane. Follow this walled lane, with a grass and hard-packed surface, slightly downhill passing through three gateways. At the fourth take a L turn down a farm track towards coniferous woodland. Take the L-hand, grassier of the two tracks, into Crookland Wood (the R-hand track is a footpath up past an old derelict farm). Turn R after 400 metres signed 'Bridleway to Derwent'. Enjoy a brief smooth gravel section then drop steeply out of the woods to cross Brook House Bridge. Turn L.

Begin climbing a path with a mixture of surfaces, initially stone pitched then sandy, up onto Delf Edge. You will soon be up on real moorland, Hingcliff Common. The track's surface varies. Though mainly of sand and rock there are also peaty sections. When you see a track veering L (in a SEterly direction) ignore it. Continue straight on until you drop down slightly to Haslingshaw before beginning a long climb up the L-hand side of Mickleden Beck.

From the open access boundary (for walkers not you!), shown on the ground by a wooden post with sign, it is a generous 2.5km to Howden Edge. Howden Edge, at 530 metres, is the high point before you begin descending. On the way up to Howden Edge, the first 1.5km is a steady climb on a loose rock/sand path. It is almost all rideable with a lot of effort, but soon the nature of the path changes. It becomes less steep and has an uneven, softer, stepped surface with rocks, peat and groughs. In wet weather this section could be very hard going with large boggy areas where some walking may be needed. When dry it is virtually all rideable.

Follow the obvious path straight on; do not go L down any groughs by mistake!

Now for some fun! You drop off the moors still on the Cut Gate path into Cranberry Clough, losing about 250 metres of height. The descent has a large variety of surfaces. There is grass, large stone slabs (recycled from mill floors) some sand, rocks, steps and large dangerous drop-offs at the bottom. You will need to get off and walk short stretches here. Take care!

Ford the stream at the bottom. Continue along to where a path from your R merges with yours. This is the footpath from Howden Moor. Go L crossing the very small wooden bridge over a stream. In front of you should be a very fine stone packhorse bridge.

Curve L, signed 'Cycle Route', climb very slightly onto a wide, 'forestry type' track with a very compact 'fast' surface. Follow it slightly downhill for about 6.5km skirting the east edge of Howden and Derwent Reservoirs. Just below Derwent Reservoir you will meet a tarmac road. Do not turn R to cross under the dam wall unless you need snacks/tea at Fairholmes car park, but continue straight on passing Jubilee Cottages and a telephone box.

About 1.6km of tarmac road leads to a well-surfaced track. Follow this for 2.5km to the Ashopton Viaduct (A57 road). Do not cross the road but turn R on the pavement/cycle path to cross the viaduct and then immediately R again. Cross the cattle grid and stay on the road for less than 600 metres before turning L to follow the very steep bridleway to, and through, Crookhill Farm.

You will probably need to do some walking here. Go through the farmyard via two gates keeping to the R. Join the track onto Crook Hill, following the R-hand wall (ignoring tracks that fork L uphill) until you come to a gate. Go through the gate and follow the wall for about 150 metres before bearing L slightly to cross open grassland (following the wooden way-marked posts).

Head for the large gate. Go through this and up the field to a bridlegate. After this there is a slightly flatter section, following wooden stakes. You should get panoramic views of Castleton, Edale and other places from this point.

On reaching another bridlegate pass through it before descending over grass to the edge of the woodland. Follow the edge of the wood to a junction of paths with several gates. You should go straight on. This sand and grass track takes you about 800 metres to a fingerpost and cross-junction of bridleways. Go straight on down the good gravel farm track. A very steep gravelly section with Z-bends takes you to Rowlee Farm to join the A57 Snake Road. Turn R.

Now follows a 7km slog, passing the Snake Inn about half way up. When you seem to be getting near the top, on one of the corners, keep an eye out for a layby and National Trust sign on the R-hand side of the road. It will say 'Doctor's Gate' and will be beside a bridlegate. Turn R here.

You are only about 7km from Glossop but this last section took us about 90 minutes. It is difficult terrain involving a lot of dismounting/remounting and some walking too. Drop down to and cross a stream. Follow the sketchy path (eroded) up from the stream and across the moors. The first 800 metres, to the point where you cross the Pennine Way, is boggy in patches but has been slabbed and stone pitched on some stretches.

Follow the old Roman road (the cobble/stone slab remains no doubt still be there buried under the new path). You will come to a point where the descent starts. It is not unlike the drop-offs and terrain back at Cut Gate but more fearsome. Take great care over the next three or four kilometers. Dismount and walk as necessary to avoid injury! From beside Rose Clough there is 1.5km of rocky track where you can only ride a short way before having to get off, walk a section and then get back on. It's very tiring.

You will cross Shelf Brook on a small wooden footbridge and continue along to the 'Open Access' boundary. Here go L onto a smoother, rideable track. Continue downhill until you meet a large metal gate. After passing through this gate you should be able to see Mossy Lea Farm on your L. Cross the small R-hand bridge and follow the track straight on, through a number of gates, past some mills and back into Glossop. Well done!

Captain Popeye fords stream, Doctor's Gate, Glossop Route

Starting the long, technical descent on Doctor's Gate

4. Ladybower

Route Details

Distance:

18 miles/29km

%age off road:

68%

Time:

4 1/2 hours

Height Gain:

605m

Map:

OS 1:25 000: Explorer
OL1 Dark Peak Area

Facilities:

Cycle hire, toilets, tea
kiosk and information at
Fairholmes

Rail Access:

Nearest station Bamford
3km if you start the route
at Heatherdene car park
(alternative start)
SK 202860

Route direction

Ladybower Reservoir, Lockerbrook
Farm, Rowlee Farm, Roman Road,
Aston, Thornhill, Derwent Moor,
Derwent, Ladybwer

Route Summary

This hilly ride, a large circle
including sections of the moors
surrounding Ladybower and
Derwent reservoirs, should give a
taste of the 'High Peak' gritstone
landscape. Though not quite
as high as the nearby Glossop,
Hayfield or Edale circles, this
very scenic route is rideable but
challenging for most riders. A
variety of tracks, paths and roads,
many of which were ancient
pack-horse routes, take you over
farmland and gritstone moorland,
through both conifer plantations
and broadleaf woodland. This
route has become a favourite for
some riders. It is fun in summer
and winter but the grit and water
combination in winter certainly
grinds away brake and gear parts.
Make sure you have good brake
pads! There are wonderful hilltop
viewpoints over the surrounding
scenery.

Start SK 173893 at Fairholmes picnic site and carpark, just below the dam wall of Derwent Reservoir. A good alternative start/finish would be the free Severn Trent car park called Heatherdene SK 202860. From Fairholmes turn R out of the car park onto the tarmac road and follow it up the W side of Derwent Reservoir for roughly 1.2km. After passing Gores Farm on your L you will curve round a L-hand corner. Just as you begin to descend take the bridleway L through a large wooden gate (no longer signposted).

Climb this steep but mostly rideable track into a conifer plantation. Well used by mountain bikes, its surface becomes a mixture of stones embedded in sand and pine needles. It is generally firm but does have some puddles and mud patches.

The track becomes less steep further up, then starts to descend slightly. As you pass Lockerbrook Farm watch out for black rabbits. Cross the stream and go through the gate before climbing a short distance up a wider track. Less than 800 metres after the farm you should come to a point where the track forks, one half curving round to the R while the other descends L.

Choose the R-hand option and cycle down the well-surfaced gravel farm track to a very steep section with Z-bends. You will come to Rowlee Farm. From here go straight across the A57 Snake Pass road and downhill on the small tarmacadam road marked with a dead-end sign. Cross over the River Ashop then climb uphill to, and through, a large gate. About 300 metres after this gate take the first L turn, a track leaving the road at an acute angle. Next is a steady climb of about 800 metres on a loose rocky surface (tricky to ride without a little walking) before descending to pass through a gateway and ford at Blackley Clough.

Go along to the next gate. From here the track is downhill on a rutted grass surface with some mud. Go straight on through the next two gates. Just after the second gate is a stone guide post,'Hope Cross'. Follow the ridge to another large gate. After this gate the track forks. You should bear L slightly, on the semi-defined path which rises gently towards the edge of the conifer plantation.

Follow this path parallel to the wood's edge, along the ridge for ca. 1.2km. You should come to a semi-derelict wall with a gateway and single stone gatepost. Only 300 metres after this look carefully for a small turn off R. There is a small cairn by it but the path is not well defined on the ground. Follow this grassy track down through a gate below Top Plantation before forking slightly R.

At the four-way fingerpost go straight on, cycling across a field (do not turn R down into the woods), then into a 'funnelling' of walls which takes you into a muddy walled lane. Pass through two gates. After the second you will come to a tarmac drive and Edge Farm. Curve R and descend to meet a road at a T-junction. Turn L. Follow this rather shady embanked lane for roughly 1.5km. Pass through the village of Aston ignoring all turns until you come to a T-junction at Thornhill. Go L signed 'Ladybower'. After only 500m downhill, just after Carr Croft and a large parking layby turn L off the road through a gap by a large gate onto a concessionary bridleway (not sign-posted). Follow this old railway line, flat with a good surface for 1km until you meet a tarmac track. Turn L uphill, climb 300 metres then walk across Ladybower Dam to meet the A6013. Turn L but stay on the pavement cycle path. Follow this across Ladybower Viaduct. Turn L at the T-junction with the A57 but still on the cycle path.

After no more than 800 metres turn R, just before Ashopton Viaduct, to cross the A57 and onto the tarmac track marked 'No Parking, No Vehicles'. Curve immediately R (do not go through the bridle gate straight ahead of you) and climb uphill past a number of houses. The surface becomes gravelly. Continue straight on to the next gate. Take the bridleway signed Cut Throat Bridge. You should be on a narrowish path which climbs gently then drops to a gate. After this gate drop to a T-junction with another track. Go L uphill through a gate with a sign saying

'Ladybower Wood Nature Reserve'. Continue riding along to cross a stream and come to another gate. After this gate you will be on a pleasant narrow moorland track amongst heather. When the track forks at a boggy patch stay R along to Cut Throat Bridge. On meeting another track turn L away from the road. Climb up onto Derwent Moor. Cycle for roughly 1.5km to a cross junction of paths at Whinstone Lee Tor. Turn R on the waymarked bridleway, slightly downhill. This path, with some boggy patches, traverses the moor just above a gritstone wall.

After about 800 metres, at the top of Grainfoot Clough, there should be a small metal sign pointing out Derwent L and Moscar R. From here turn L through the gate and descend to a bridlegate. Go through the gate and continue down the path as it follows the R-hand edge of the plantation. Drop down to a ford.

After the ford the bridleway goes through a large gate between two very old small barns. Take a peek in the R-hand barn with the curlew bench. Turn L through a narrow gateway onto a very steep grass hill. Follow the stone-slabbed path down until you meet a hard track beside the reservoir.

Turn R onto this track. Ride along the E edge of the reservoir. You will curve L and cross Mill Brook then soon reach a small tarmac road. About 1.2km along this road you will reach a post box and Jubilee Cottages. Just past this point keep following the tarmac road (rather than the track) to curve L below the wall of Derwent Dam back to your starting point.

Opposite: Both illustrations above Ladybower

5. Stanage

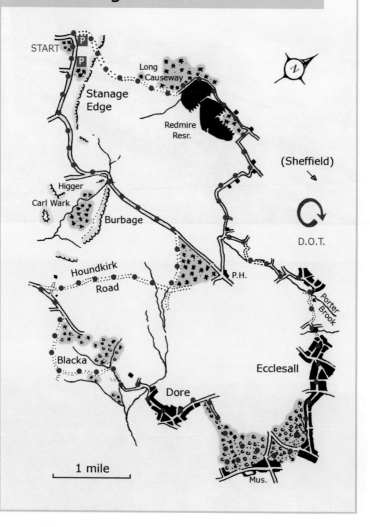

START

P
P

Stanage Edge

Long Causeway

Redmire Resr.

(Sheffield)

D.O.T.

Higger

Carl Wark

Burbage

Houndkirk Road

Blacka

P.H.

Porter Brook

Ecclesall

Dore

Mus.

1 mile

Route Details

Distance:

23 miles/37km

%age off road:

52%

Time:

5 hours

Height Gain:

580m

Map:

Mostly on OS Explorer OL1
Dark Peak Area, or all on
1:50 000 Landranger 110
Sheffield

Facilities:

Pubs and shops in Ecclesall,
pubs at Dore and near
Houndkirk Moor

Rail Access:

Bamford Station 2.5km
from start

Route 5. Stanage

Route direction

Long Causeway, Stanage Edge,
Ecclesall, Ecclesall Wood, Dore,
Blacka Plantation, Houndkirk
Road, Burbage Moor, Dennis
Knoll, Long Causeway Circle.

Route Summary

This is a great, varied ride, quite
hilly and tough. It starts on the
moors N of Hathersage, below the
imposing Stanage Edge, a long
gritstone edge usually dotted
with climbers and walkers. Then
it passes over moorland and
touches the edge of Sheffield,
sneaking through some lovely
mixed woodland (especially fine
in the spring with bluebells, fresh
beech leaves and really big oaks).

Away from Sheffield the route
again crosses sandy moorland on
well-compacted but bumpy paths,
before a fast road section back
under Stanage Edge to finish.
This route would be OK to ride in
reverse direction but is better as
described.

Start SK227843 (parking laybys) by Dennis Knoll. Ride Nwards up the rough track that leaves the road at the sharp corner after a cattle grid. This track, the 'Long Causeway', is a rough technical climb (about 1.5km) to Stanedge Pole. It is mainly a rock-strewn sand track so although often wet it should not be too muddy. It is suffering a bit from heavy use by 4-wheel drive users. It curves onto the Edge, follows the top a short way then curves Ewards to a high point of 438m at Stanedge Pole.

From here ride down the rutted bumpy track towards Redmires Reservoirs passing through the gate part-way down. Turn L at the bottom of the hill onto Redmires Road and follow this round the N side of the reservoirs. From here you will be able to see the city of Sheffield sprawled below you. After less than 800 metres of descent, as you begin to climb again, take the first road R, Soughley Lane. Take the next R by Peat Farm. This road zigzags steeply uphill then levels out before dropping downhill. You want the second road L, about 1.5km from Peat Farm, called Greenhouse Lane (just after a pebble-dashed house). There is a blue cycle sign saying 'City Centre'.

Now 500 metres down Greenhouse Lane the road bends 90 degrees L. You should leave the tarmac here by continuing straight on (blue City Centre cycle sign). Follow this rough walled track, Clough Lane as it descends steeply, crosses a footpath and then Porter Brook. Follow the brook for a while before joining a small tarmac road. Ignore the road L, ride straight on then take a signed bridleway L. After 100 metres cross the road, go through the bridlegate and follow the well-surfaced path. Soon rejoin tarmac by some large stone houses. Turn R then immediately R again onto the signed bridleway that climbs to Whiteley Wood Road. Turn L onto the road but then take the first R after only 100 metres, onto the waymarked byway just above the farm. Ford the stream and ride up the track into a residential area.

You will be on Trap Lane and should follow it, ignoring any turn-offs until you meet a larger road just opposite Bents Green Methodist Church. From here turn R, then immediately L onto Knowle Lane (which is the road just below the church). Take the first turn onto Harley Road. Ride down here, straight across the next two crossroads onto Dobcroft Road. After roughly 750 metres you should reach a zebra crossing and a road turning L. Immediately opposite this is a signposted bridleway between two houses which is very difficult to see. Turn R down this bridleway signed 'Bridleway to Whirlowdale Road' into lovely mature mixed woodland, a real 'green lung' for the city.

This is Ecclesall Wood, which has a number of footpaths and bridleways. Follow the blue arrows and signs to Whirldale Road crossing two streams and, when the path forks, stay L. You will soon meet a road and should go straight across to re-enter the wood on the lower of the two paths. Follow the blue arrowed bridleway signed Abbeydale Rd. On meeting a second road go almost straight across, using not the stile but the wooden gate below it. Follow the well-surfaced bridleway to Abbeydale Rd.

You should come out on the road opposite the end of the millpond (there is a museum, open to the public on certain days, called Abbeydale Industrial Museum, on the far side of the road). Go back into the woods uphill on the bridleway signposted Limb Lane. It may be difficult to distinguish your path but stick to the most substantial path which curves L, skirts up inside the L-hand edge of the wood and crosses Limb Brook.

After crossing the brook turn R following the signs 'Bridleway to Dore'. The path climbs slightly uphill through an area dominated by Scots Pine. Go up the stretch of walled lane to a road called Limb Lane. Go L here towards Townsend, continuing on the road until you meet a road junction, (a slightly offset cross-roads). Go straight across onto High Street then first R opposite the Hare and Hounds pub. You are on Townhead Road. This is a good spot for dinner with a pub and shops.

After refreshment head up the road through the residential area before descending steeply to cross Redcar Brook. About 100 metres after this turn L onto Shorts Lane, waymarked as a bridleway. Ride down this hard compacted track curving sharply R at the bottom, to follow 'Bridleway to Blacka Moor ' signs. Continue descending and fork R to follow the signs rather than crossing the stream.

After a stone gateway follow the well-surfaced narrow path beside the stream until it splits just before another gateway with stone post. Bear L to ford the stream then climb more steeply (Blacka Dike). It is a good path through mixed woodland (mainly oak, elder, alder and birch) with noisy streams nearby. Some walking will probably be needed. On meeting a T-junction of bridleways at the wall turn R uphill. This rough track goes through a gate, climbs over rough grassland and passes between two stone pillars. Continue up here through another gate and along the compacted track to join the busy Hathersage Road. Turn L onto the road.

After 800 metres ignore the road off L to Calver and Bakewell. About 500 metres down the hill you will see a track signposted 'Parson House Farm'. Do not take this but take the next R soon after it which leaves the road at an acute angle. This undulating sand and rock track is Houndkirk Road which crosses Burbage and Houndkirk moors. After 200 metres go straight over the farm track and through a gate. Follow the good track for about 2.5km. You will cross Sparkinson's Spring then, after another 400 metres, you will drop slightly into a second stream clough. At this point another track crosses yours. Turn L.

If you come to the edge of the plantation and a wooden five-bar gate before turning L you have missed the turning so go back slightly. The L-hand turn also takes you to the plantation edge but to the W edge which it follows all the way to Ringinglow Road. Go L onto the road and ride about 2.5km, passing over Upper Burbage Bridge (Higger Tor, Carl Wark and Burbage Edge are all down to your L) before taking the road R (cattlegrid). An enjoyable downhill follows but you want the first R after 1km. This road takes you along below Stanage Edge and back to your starting point. Relax!

Below: Descending on the Stanage Causway

Above: Resting up near top

6. Castleton

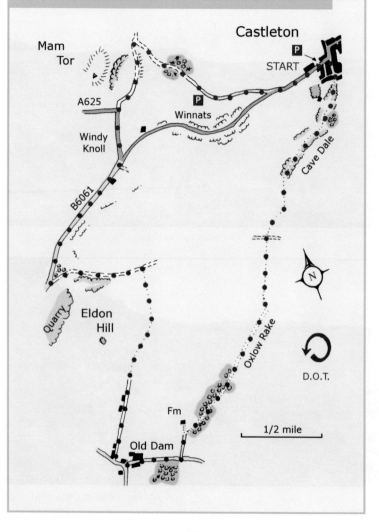

Castleton

Mam Tor

A625

Winnats

Windy Knoll

B6061

Cave Dale

START

Eldon Hill

Quarry

Oxlow Rake

N

Fm

D.O.T.

Old Dam

1/2 mile

Route Details

Distance:
9 miles/14.5km

%age off road:
67%

Time:
2 hours

Height Gain:
390m

Map:
OS 1:25 000 Explorer,
OL1 Dark Peak Area and
OL 24 White Peak (west)
split between both maps!

Facilities:
Shops, cafes, pubs, tourist
information, toilets in
Castleton

Rail Access:
Hope station 3.2km

Route direction

Mam Tor, Windy Knoll, Eldon
Hill Quarry, Old Dam, Oxlow
Rake, Cave Dale, Castleton

Route Summary

This short ride is mainly well
drained and easy going, on
roads, hard tracks and grass,
with a final fun descent down
a narrow rocky limestone
dale. It would make a pleasant
summer's evening ride. If you
wanted to make a day or two's
trip, the Castleton area has
plenty of other off-road rides to
try as well as attractions such
as show caves, good climbing
and walking, pubs and cafes.
But be warned, it is a favourite
tourist spot.

Start SK149829 at the carpark in Castleton. Leave the carpark and turn R up the road. When the Winnats Pass Road forks L, you should curve R on the old Mam Tor road. This passes the entrance to Treak Cliff Cavern and a layby which could offer an alternative starting point.

Go through the gate by Odin Mine. Follow the old subsiding road beneath Mam Tor (avoiding the tarmac crevasses) to join the B6061. This dramatic start feels rather like riding in a country suffering from earthquakes.

From here follow the Sparrowpit signs, along the road. You want the first bridleway L after 2km, just before the ever-expanding Eldon Hill Quarry. This sharp L takes you back along a stone track past both the quarry and a large gate on your R. Almost at the top of the hill turn R (due S) through a metal bridlegate next to a wall.

The bridleway initially follows the L-hand wall. Then it leaves the wall diagonally, climbs very slightly to join a grass vehicle-width track (by a post) that contours round the tumulus (ancient burial mound). Soon you drop to join a farm track at another gate. Ride down the farm track past the farm. Turn L and then L again which should take you up Old Dam Lane. After 500 metres of gentle climbing on tarmac turn next L. This leads to Oxlow End and takes you beside a farm. Turn R through the gate onto Oxlow Rake and climb up the track through the woods.

Follow the track with Oxlow Rake (depressions, humps and bumps) to your L until, roughly 1.6km from where you joined this track below the woods, while heading downhill, you come to another gate. Another bridleway from Starvehouse Mine joins yours from the R. Bear L to cross over the rake. Follow the L-hand field edge to a junction of tracks with a number of gates.

Choose the bridleway to Castleton (which is straight on). It goes across fields to Cave Dale. After 600 metres a footpath which looks the more substantial of the two choices forks L and heads very slightly uphill but you should bear R through a narrow wooden gate. Win Hill, a conical hill a few km away, should be visible straight ahead of you in clear weather.

After the second small gate the fun starts with a very technical rocky downhill section which should test both your wheels and your trails skills. Anything from a dozen or so judicious dabs with one foot to a stretch of walking may be needed here. Once through the pleasant steep-sided Cave Dale (NOTE, this bridleway is heavily used by walkers) you are soon back in Castleton. You will emerge on a small road.

There is an option of a link with the Bradwell Circle from here, see detail below. Riding down the road then turning L should bring you back to your starting point.

CASTLETON / BRADWELL LINK

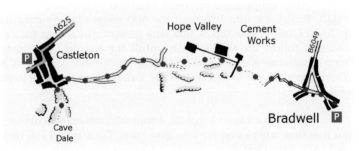

The start/finish points of the Castleton/Bradwell circular routes are approx. 3km apart. They combine well to make a good day's ride. We suggest starting with the Castleton Circle then doing the Bradwell Circle before finishing back in Castleton.

From the end of the Castleton Route to the start/finish point of the Bradwell Route:

When you emerge from Cave Dale and meet the small road in Castleton turn R. After 400 metres, when the road forks, go L. Nearly 800 metres along this undulating road is a sharp L-hand corner. Cross almost straight over through a small gate and onto a bridleway just below a large track. This good bridleway is well waymarked and will take you straight through Hope Valley cement works. Beware of large lorries and other machinery.

Roughly 800 metres along here, after a short but steep climb you will meet a farm track and turn L. Descend the walled path to meet a road junction in Bradwell. Go straight across the small road and down Town Lane to meet the B6049. Turn R and the car park start point for the Bradwell Circuit is about 300 metres along here on your L.

From the end of Bradwell to the start/finish of the Castleton Route:

After dropping down from Bradwell Edge, turn R onto the B6049. Ride back into Bradwell for 500 metres before turning L up Town Lane. At the top of this lane go straight across the small road and follow the walled path uphill for roughly 400 metres. Turn R onto the waymarked bridleway signposted 'Castleton' and follow this all the way through Hope Valley cement works to meet a road.

At the road turn L uphill. About 800 metres will bring you to a junction where you have to give way. Turn R and follow this road back into Castleton. Curve R to pass the Youth Hostel and join the A625 in Castleton. Turn L back to your Castleton Circuit start/finish point.

Opposite: above Cave Dale with Peveril Castle top left and below on the landslide broken road with Mam Tor in the background

7. Bradwell

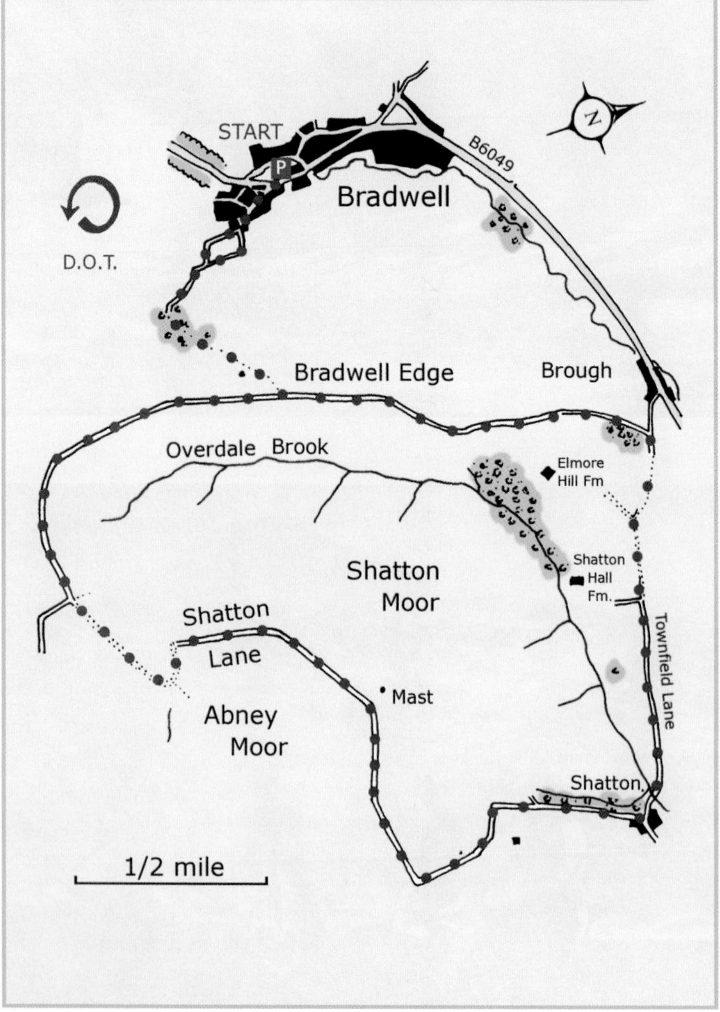

START

P

Bradwell

B6049

N

D.O.T.

Bradwell Edge

Brough

Overdale Brook

Elmore
Hill Fm

Shatton
Moor

Shatton
Hall
Fm.

Shatton
Lane

Townfield Lane

• Mast

Abney
Moor

Shatton

1/2 mile

Route Details

Distance:

6 miles/9.5km

%age off road:

83%

Time:

2 hours

Height Gain:

513m

Map:

OS 1:25 000 Explorer OL1
Dark Peak Area

Facilities:

Pubs and shops in Bradwell

Rail Access:

Bamford station is less than
8km if you start the route in
Shatton (Wheat Hay Farm)
SK 199823

Route direction

Bradwell Edge, Shatton Lane,
Shatton, Brough, Bradwell
Edge, Bradwell.

Route Summary

This is another short ride in
the Castleton, Hope area. A
stiff climb takes you up onto
Bradwell Edge where there is
open moorland and great views
of the surrounding area. It is
not unusual to see hang-gliders
or hard winged gliders (from
the nearby Great Hucklow
gliding club) overhead. A circle
of the moors on well-drained
wide tracks with fast descents
and short, steep climbs will
bring you back to this edge.
Then you return to Bradwell
down the path you laboured up
initially.

Start SK174813 at the public, parish carpark in Bradwell, next to the 'Co-op' shop. Turn L out of the car park onto the B6049, pass the church on your L and you will soon see the Shoulder of Mutton pub to your R. Opposite this pub is a small road off L – take it. Ahead some pedestrian steps should be visible. Follow the road as it curves R, then dog-legs back to reach the top of these steps. You are about to start a very steep but short climb of roughly 180m height gain to Bradwell Edge. There are cottages on your L and soon a road forks off uphill to the R. Ignore it and follow Bessie Lane as it drops into a dip.

Ignoring the second fork R, climb out of the dip. You should now be at a point with a fingerpost and two options, L or R. Go R on tarmac until a newish house. If you go L you reach a field gateway where you bear R up a narrow overgrown path. (The two meet higher up the hill where the surface becomes loose gravel.)

Continue uphill. The path, between scrub, soon becomes narrow. As you go through the small wooden gate beside a stile you will notice it is becoming very steep. Some walking will no doubt be in order. The path at first follows the R-hand fence then winds its way up the hill. One consolation is you will later be riding down here. When the path forks, take the bridleway L just above a gritstone wall. The next section is rideable, so continue following the old wall up to Bradwell Edge.

On meeting another fence/wall at the top of the ridge curve abruptly R and follow this wall along the top of the hill for roughly 100 metres to a small metal gate on your L. Go through this gate, cross the field and turn R onto the gravel track. This track (Brough Lane) sweeps round in a large gentle L-hand curve above the head of Over Dale.

After about 1.6km you should come to a junction where a road to the R drops down to Abney and a footpath goes off L. Carry straight on along the RUPP which is a grassy but still wide track signposted 'Bridleway to Shatton 2 miles'.

After roughly 400 metres curve L at the point where another fingerpost says 'Bridleway to Shatton' and a footpath leaves to the R. Soon you curve R, join a walled track and go through a gate onto Shatton Lane. You have now got 2.4km of steep downhill to come but care should be taken since there is a loose gravel surface and a gate part way down. To your L slightly, in the distance you may be able to see the bottom of Ladybower Reservoir.

Go past the large TV/Radio mast on your L, down to and through the gate, opening it first! There is a sharp corner L then the road drops very steeply. Take the first road L by Wheat Hay Farm, ride through the ford and follow Townfield Lane towards Brough.

After 800 metres the road disappears and the drive forks L to Shatton Hall Farm (Upper Shatton on O.S. map). Fork R on the good track, along the L edge of one field. Ignore a second track left to Elmore Hill Farm, go straight on through the gate and down the short steep descent to join a road on a hairpin corner.

Turn L and climb uphill. The surface soon becomes stony. Continue up this stiff climb for about 1.2km, until you are at the point where you joined this track from Bradwell Edge earlier in the ride. Look for the metal gate on your R just after a track drops gently to the L. Turn R through the large gate, go across to, and through the small metal gate.

Follow the bridleway (you struggled up earlier) down into Bradwell. Take care on the steep descent. Finish at the pub for sustenance.

8. Buxton

Taxal

Fm.

Ladder
Hill

Fernilee Resr.

A5004

1 mile

White
Hall

D.O.T.

START

P

Roman Road

Errwood
Resr.

P

P

Buxton

Old Road

P Derbyshire Bridge

Route Details

Distance:

15 miles/24km

%age off road:

60%

Time:

3 hours

Height Gain:

225m

Map:

OS 1:25 000 Explorer
OL24 White Peak (west)

Facilities:

Pubs and shops in Bradwell

Rail Access:

Shops,cafes and pubs and
cycle shop in Buxton
Rail Access: Buxton Station
800 metres if you start the
route in Buxton on the (A53)

Route direction

Errwood Reservoir, Goyt's
Clough, Derbyshire Bridge,
Macclesfield Road, Buxton,
Roman Road, Ladder Hill,
Taxal, Hoo Moor, Errwood
Reservoir.

Route Summary

Buxton is high up and can be
cold in winter. It is usually one
of the first places in Derbyshire
to get snow. This is a really nice
route with little traffic. Both
varied and hilly it starts in the
Goyt valley. It skirts Buxton
and sweeps in a large circle
back to Taxal and then through
Hoo Moor plantation to the
reservoirs. There can be a few
boggy patches but generally
surfaces are suitable for most
weather conditions. On a clear
day there are fine views from
the hilltops of both Kinder to
the east and over the Cheshire
Plain to the west.

Start at Errwood Reservoir SK 102748 although other possible starting points would be: Buxton, Whaley Bridge or the picnic site close to Derbyshire Bridge.

Assuming you start at Errwood, turn R out of the carpark and begin the long steady climb up the road towards Derbyshire Bridge. There are rewarding views over Goyt's Moss, Burbage Edge and into Goyt's Clough. After passing over the tiny Derbyshire Bridge you will approach the carpark and picnic site. Turn L off the narrow road and continue climbing on a compacted track signposted 'Path 6 Berry Clough, Buxton', keeping the car park to your R.

This well-surfaced track is the old Macclesfield road. It will take you across open moorland. Climb roughly 1.2km to the high point of the route then descend into the Burbage area of Buxton, passing through a gate as you do so (with the old High Peak railway to your L).

Back on tarmac, you soon meet the A53 Leek road at the main crossroads by Christchurch. Turn L onto the A53. Freewheel about 800 metres down into Buxton and as the hill flattens out slightly take the L-hand turn signposted 'Cavendish Golf Club' (Carlisle Road). Climb up this road to meet a T-junction. Turn L here, then on meeting the very busy A5004 Whaley Bridge road turn L again. Climb away from Buxton for roughly 800 metres. After passing Cold Springs Farm on your L the road bends sharply to the L. Leave the road here, by crossing with great care to fork R on a track (signed dead end and byway) which technically is almost 'straight on'. This narrow roadway was once a Roman road linking Buxton with more northerly towns and forts.

Climbing steeply, at first on tarmac, the track takes you over typical Peak moorland. It's an upland grazing area so do not forget to close gates behind you. After this climb you then descend past Whitehall Outdoor Centre and mountain rescue post following the track as it curves to the R. Continue straight on, ignoring the road that drops R towards Combs, and you should find yourself climbing up the tarmac road towards the natural gap in the ridge at Wainstones. From here, as you descend, take the first R forking off the road at Wythen Lache Farm. Go through the gate and into a walled lane which can be muddy.

After the second gateway the track crosses open fields and is badly rutted. It will take you quickly down to another narrow tarmac road above Thorny Lee. Turn L and down the steep hill with caution. At the sharp R-hand bend in the road turn L into a walled lane (Long Lane). Climb up and traverse around Ladder Hill (on top of which is a TV mast). The steep stony track soon levels out. The surface becomes sandy and there are excellent views north over Chapel, with Kinder Scout forming the horizon.

Drop downhill on this rough track. At the next road junction turn R and ride down past Elnor Lane Farm. Turn R at the first T-junction and go down the road. Take the second road L by houses, a telephone box and post box. This should be Shallcross Road. Ride to the end of this road. It narrows and passes some new houses on the L. Curve R slightly down a steep rutted track which will deposit you on the A5004 just outside Whaley Bridge.

Cross with care into the large layby opposite. Roughly halfway along this layby is an opening in the wall which leads onto a steep track into the wood. Take this, dog-leg round the corner and ford the River Goyt at the bottom, (riders without webbed feet can use the bridge). A very steep, but thankfully short climb takes you between the graveyards of St. James Church into Taxal.

At the top of this climb turn L along the narrow road, mostly uphill to Overton Hall Farm. At the farm turn L. The track (now tarmac) drops steeply, bends and twists down to the stream passing a small farm on the way. Cross the stream in Mill Clough. Climb up the path away from the stream for 250 metres. Just before Knipe Farm, on the brow you should head off R, through a gate in the wire fence onto grass fields. Still uphill, the path across the fields stays close to the L-hand edge (bounded by a plantation). Pass through the next gate and dog-leg L up the walled bridleway. Go through a gate to pass barns and a stable, keeping to the lower of the two tracks. Cycle along to another gateway and Oldfield Farm. Pass quietly through the farmyard, then take the upper track leading into Forestry Commission woodland, waymarked 'Hoo Moor and Erwood'

Above, looking down on Bradwell, catching some breath

     The next 1.6km is a well surfaced gravel forestry track. At the end of the wood, where you meet a tarmac road, turn L and enjoy a very fine smooth downhill. Curve R at the bottom to follow the edge of Errwood reservoir back to your starting point.

Tom and Monty - on route maintenance

Oxlow Rake, Castleton Route

9. Chelmorton

Limestone Way

Monks Dale

Monksdale Fm.

N

Wormhill

Tunstead

Chee Dale

D.O.T.

Blackwell Dale

Mosley Fm.

Tunstead Quarry

A6

P.H.

START P

Topley Pike

River Wye

Deep Dale

King Sterndale

(Buxton)

Chelmorton

Priests Way

1 mile

Route Details

Distance:

15 miles/24km

%age off road:

76%

Time:

3 1/2 hours

Height Gain:

477m

Map:

OS 1:25 000 Explorer OL24
White Peak Area

Facilities:

Pubs on route

Rail Access:

Buxton station 4km

Route direction

Topley Pike, Wye Dale, King
Sterndale, Horseshoe Dale,
Chelmorton, Limestone Way,
Miller's Dale, Limestone Way,
Wormhill, Wye Dale.

Route Summary

A real variety both of surfaces
and scenery is offered by this
ride. There are steep-sided
scenic limestone dales, gravel
tracks, green roads, bridleways,
stretches of walled lanes (the
'Limestone Way') and complex
patterns of walled fields around
Chelmorton. The high ground
can be a little exposed if it is
windy. Some sections of this
route are muddy so perhaps
avoid it in very wet weather.
There are plenty of ups and
downs and a little walking so
allow yourself plenty of time.
A deceptively tough ride for
its length, especially in wet
weather.

Start in the Monsal Trail car park off the main A6 Buxton, Bakewell road (opposite Topley Pike quarry entrance) SK 104725. This can get very busy especially at weekends, as it is a popular car park for the northern end of the Monsal Trail. Turn R onto the A6. Follow it for roughly 800 metres then go L on a track marked 'Unsuitable for Motors' (opposite a stone bridge across the river). It heads diagonally back up a steep hill at an acute angle to the road.

This rideable gravel track curves R, flattens out and enters King Sterndale by a stone cross and the village green. After another 800 metres the now tarmacked road curves R, but we take the waymarked track straight on through a small wood (Horsestone Hill Plantation) and gate onto grass fields. Do not follow the footpath which hugs the wall to your R. Instead go through the gate and across the field diagonally on an undefined path, aiming for a gate slightly to the R of the fence dividing the two lower fields.

Cross the next field diagonally too. You will see a small gate. Go through this and you will be in an area of rough tussocky grass. There is a steep drop on one side of you into Deep Dale so take care. Ride a short way parallel to, but above, the dale before dropping down the path which has a sharp L-hand bend at the bottom. Go through the small gate in front of you and follow 'Priest's Way' up the small but attractive Horseshoe Dale (not Back Dale immediately R). There are some tricky mud and rock areas around the gateways. After passing through a farm, you should join the A5270. Go L and follow the undulating road for nearly 1.6km, ignoring the two R turns to Chelmorton. Further up this road, at the top of a rise, you will see the end of two stone houses (Arden Villas) on your L. 200 metres past these, on your R, go through a second gate just next to a drystone wall (opposite a footpath fingerpost). This is an undefined grass bridleway which you follow as it contours round under Chelmorton Low, just above the limestone wall.

After one field go through another large gate. Keep following the R-hand wall. This section can be very muddy. You will reach a small bridlegate in the R-hand wall below a large sycamore tree. Go through the gate; Chelmorton Church will now be straight in front of you and the Church Inn just below you. Turn L and climb up the track which soon levels out. You will ride along a rake, over slag from the old open-mine workings. On meeting a bridlegate turn L onto a wide gravel track, Follow this for 400 metres. Go through a large gate then ride down the rutted track. After another large gate turn R onto tarmac but when, in a few hundred metres the track turns 90 degrees L, go straight on following the non-tarmac Senners Lane along to the A6. Turn R, then take a L turn opposite the Waterloo Hotel down Priestcliffe Road.

At the next cross-roads turn L. Then as the road curves L, watching carefully for traffic, take the track straight on. This is the Limestone Way (Long Lane). It is a steep descent. Watch out for potholes and walkers. On meeting the road turn R down to Miller's Dale. Ignore the first road L and continue along the road under the huge steel railway bridges. After a church take the small but very steep road uphill to the L. After less than 150 metres turn L again on the bridleway (Limestone Way) into the woods then L through Monksdale Farm.

Follow this walled lane which can be muddy. After about 1.2km, at the fork, turn L. Ride along the walled lane to a road and Monksdale House. Turn L. A steep downhill and sharp bend are followed by more uphill. Pass a footpath on your L. Less than 150 metres from the bottom of the hill go L through the large wooden gate marked 'Pennine Bridleway Wormhill three quarters of a mile' onto an undefined bridleway, up and across the field aiming for the top L-hand corner. At the top of the field is a small gate into a walled lane. Follow this uphill. After a small gate take the R fork. At the next junction go R again through a large gate and continue along the walled lane.

On meeting the road at Wormhill turn R then immediately L, up through Old Hall Farm, following Pennine Bridleway. Pass through the farmyard bearing slightly L to pass through a large gate (normally open) onto a stony track. Follow this along the L-hand side of a wall. Drop downhill, then go through the R-hand gate, following the path with a wall to your L, to the road and turn L.

Go past some quarry houses and stay on tarmac as the road curves L. After about 300 metres the road rises slightly. Stay on tarmac for the next 1km until you see a small wooden bridlegate on the L. Take this onto a walled grass lane. After only 200 metres, go R cross the tarmac, through a bridlegate and follow the R-hand edge of one field to a walled lane. Turn L, go through the next large metal gate. Turn R to pass above Mosley Farm then just after the farm turn L signed 'Pennine Bridleway to Chee Dale' down a zigzag grass track, which drops dramatically into Chee Dale. Waah! watch you don't over-shoot any corners!

Pass under the old railway (arched bridge), down to the river. Follow it upstream then cross the river in front of a row of houses, by ford or foot- bridge. Follow the track upstream parallel to the river about 800 metres back to the carpark start point.

Opposite, Horseshoe Dale

10. Baslow

Great Hucklow

Peters
Dale

Silly
Dale

Wardlow

Grindlow

A623

1 mile

Y.H.A.
P.H.

Bretton

N

High
Rake

Eyam

Rowland

Stoney
Middleton

Hassop

Calver

River
Derwent

A619

Curbar

Baslow

START P

P

D.O.T.

Route Details

Distance:

22 miles/35km

%age off road:

55%

Time:

4 hours

Height Gain:

723m

Map:

OS 1:25 000 Explorer
OL24 White Peak Area

Facilities:

Shops and cafe at both
Baslow and Eyam

Rail Access:

If you join the route at Sir
William Hill SK 224780
Grindleford station is only
4km from here.

Route direction

Baslow, Hassop, Rowland,
High Rake, Wardlow Mires,
Grindlow, Great Hucklow,
Eyam, Stoney Middleton,
Calver, Baslow Edge, Baslow.

Route Summary

This excellent all-weather route
is mainly formed by cunningly
linked pieces of unclassified
road. It is a good route for cafe
stops. Also there are villages
with historical interest. Eyam
is noted for its architecture and
for its selfless restraint when
the Plague swept through the
village in the 17th century.

Start in Baslow at the Park Side public carpark SK 258721. Turn L out of the carpark. Go L at the roundabout (signposted Bakewell, Buxton, Chatsworth, Rowsley, Haddon). Then take the second proper road R which is signposted 'Bakewell A619, Buxton A6'. Nearly 1.5km up this road, on your R, above a stream, you will see a large gate with a sign saying 'Unsuitable for Motors'.

Go through this gate and along a well-surfaced track. You should be able to see a small stone barn ahead of you with four arched windows. Follow the track through the wood, ignoring a track L uphill, then descend to ford a small stream and climb gently up a narrower walled path. You will pass through about three gates before coming to the road at Hassop.

Turn R, then just round the corner take the first road L (signposted Great Longstone and Rowland) past the opulent entrance to Hassop Hall. Follow it for 1.2km. It climbs uphill then levels. Take the first road signposted 'Rowland Only'. Ride up through the village and past Top Farm. The tarmac gives way to a gravel track and there is a welcome 'Unsuitable for Motors' sign. Continuing up this track you should be able to see the curved wall of an underground reservoir above you, to your R.

Go straight on following this vehicle-width track as it climbs steadily for the next 1.5 km ignoring any paths off L. It flattens out and you will cross a cattlegrid at a gateway. When the track forks go L and after 100 metres L again. Climb slightly uphill following the edge of a long thin wood on your L and the filled-in rake (High Rake) on your R. After 1 km turn R through the metal bridlegate (opposite the entrance to Bleaklow Farm). Cross the rake and go through the wooden bridlegate onto a grass/dirt track.

Follow this bridleway as it climbs gently and curves L to another gate. Pass through this and slither down the rutted, walled, green lane, to reach a wide quarry track. Cross this, go straight on through the wide bridlegate (immediately cross another bridleway) and follow the track ahead along and then uphill.

You should be on the L of two gravel tracks running side by side. Curve R uphill. When two tracks merge, remain on the L-hand track which skirts along the edge of a huge 'sludge lagoon'. On meeting a small road, turn R, again R and almost immediately L down tarmac into Wardlow. Turn R at the T-junction. Ride down to the busy A623 road at Wardlow Mires and at the A623 turn L signposted Stockport and Manchester. Peter's Stone is on your L. Take the next road R. It is only very small and signposted 'Access Only'. Take care turning off the main road, you are in a dip, hidden from fast-moving traffic.

Once on the small road (Trot Lane) you drop into a dip, curve L and climb slightly. Take the R turn towards Stanley House marked with a dead-end sign. At Stanley House the tarmac disappears and you should turn 90 degrees L on a stony track. This track has limestone walls on either side, twisting and bulging as if ready to collapse any minute. They will probably stay like that for 50 years! These drystone walls, typical of the area, stretch for miles, surrounding fields that are by today's standards very small. The track narrows as it branches L to run parallel with Silly Dale. Follow it to a road junction where you should go straight across towards Grindlow.

Pass through Grindlow on the road. Turn R at the T-junction near Great Hucklow, to follow a signpost saying 'Gliding Club and Bretton'. It is uphill again, but is rideable! After less than 800 metres there is a road L signposted 'Gliding Club and Abney'. Ignore this but ride straight on uphill (it then flattens) for the next 1.5km until you pass Bretton Youth Hostel on your L. You should then turn L immediately before the Barrel Inn. This downhill track curves R and offers good views left out towards Bretton Clough.

The tarmac is soon replaced by a stony surface and you climb about 800 metres to come out at a road, again on a corner.

Turn immediately L onto the gravel track marked 'Unsuitable for Motors' and follow it over Broad low and Sir William Hill, passing a large aerial. Ride down a straight section to meet the Eyam to Grindleford road. Bear R onto this road towards Eyam.

You will pass the famous Mompesson's Well then should turn R towards Highcliffe (signposted 'Bretton, Abney and Great Hucklow'). 800 metres along this road you will come to Highcliffe Farm. Turn L opposite the farm to follow a steep mud and rock track.

This winding unclassified road descends steeply into the village of Eyam. On reaching the road proper, on a corner, turn R. Ride downhill past the carpark, then go L on the road to Town End, passing Eyam Hall on the way. Several roads converge at Town End, which could be considered the centre of Eyam village. There are a number of shops including several cafes.

Immediately below (or above) Eyam Tea Rooms turn R. These two tarmac tracks/roads merge. Follow the tarmac road to a farm. Go L down the track beside the farm in roughly a SE direction. Tarmac soon peters out as this pleasant unclassified road descends towards Stoney Middleton. Pass through two gates as necessary. On reaching the main road (A623) at Stoney Middleton turn L and follow it about 2km to Calver, passing straight ahead at the traffic lights.

The next road left says 'Calver Mill'. Take this option then curve R to cross the River Derwent. Immediately after the bridge are two L turns, the first to Froggatt and the second, which you want, to Curbar village.

There is now a snorter of a hill up through Curbar Village, to Curbar Gap. It is the point at which the road passes between the dramatic Curbar and Baslow gritstone edges (part of a chain of such edges that runs down the eastern flank of the Peak). At the top of the hill is a carpark on your L. Just before this go R through one of the bridlegates onto Baslow Edge. Savour the view. You have earned it! Follow the larger L-hand track (bridleway) along Baslow Edge until there is a track turning R. At this point you will be able to see Wellington's Monument (a stone cross) a little further on to your L. You will need to go down the track to the R (however if you wish, you could ride along the rest of the edge, before returning to this point.).

Near Baslow Edge

Eventually descend the rough, steep track into Baslow, passing through a gate as necessary. At the main road in Baslow turn L and follow it to your starting point.

11. Linacre

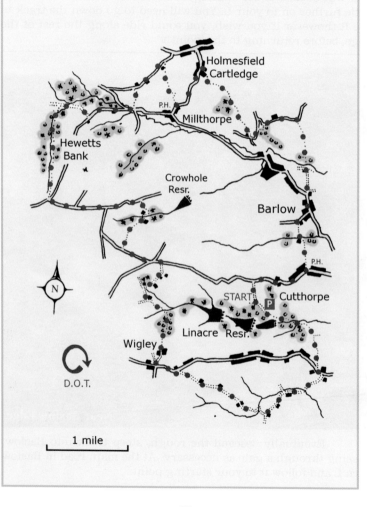

Route Details

Distance:

17.5 miles/28km

%age off road:

65%

Time:

4 1/2 hours

Height Gain:

780m

Map:

O.S. 1:25 000 Explorer
OL24 White Peak Area

Facilities:

Pubs at Milnthorpe,
Holmesfield, Barlow and
Cutthorpe

Rail Access:

Nearest station Chesterfield,
2.4km if you start at Ashgate
Hospice

Route 11. Linacre

Route direction

Linacre Reservoirs, Ashgate,
Riddings, Wigley, Birley,
Moorhall, Hewetts Bank,
Horsleygate, Cartledge, Barlow,
Cutthorpe, Linacre Reservoirs.

Route Summary

Linacre Reservoirs are
surrounded by mature mixed
woodland. There are two
nature trail walks of 1.km
and 3.2km. Our cycle route
links interesting stretches of
bridleway often used by horses.
It is a fun and challenging ride
with lots of ups and downs
plus a number of streams to
cross, and some muddy and wet
singletrack. The countryside
is dotted with reservoirs,
quite large areas of land being
owned by the water authority.
In clear weather the hilltops
give panoramic views of the
surrounding area which means
you can look back on the
stretch of route you have just
covered.

The tracks, generally not too rocky tend to be either sand and gravel farm tracks or narrow muddy paths; some doubling as streams. Stretches of this route do get very muddy but we have tried to arrange it so that these are downhill. Even in very wet weather you shouldn't have to walk more than 1km in all.

There is now a concessionary bridleway around the middle of the three Linacre reservoirs. It only takes about 10 minutes to ride but is worth cycling around before you start your route if you would like a view of the mixed woodland and dam wall. Go in at the gate just above the toilet block and Ranger base and follow the blue arrows on a well-surfaced wide track along the north side of the middle reservoir. Go up to and across the dam wall of the top reservoir, back down through the woods, and cross the dam wall of the middle reservoir to your starting track.

Start at one of the three Linacre carparks SK 336728. Turn out of one of the carparks away from the road you came in on, onto the bridleway towards Ashgate. Downhill, in a SE direction, it is at first a tarmac surface but soon becomes a wide track of mud and stone. Cross Linacre Brook and continue straight on (ignore the bridleway R) cycling alongside the stream, then follow this track as it climbs out of the woods and passes Woodnook Cottage. Ignore both the small footpath that veers off L and the track L to the housing estate. Follow the track you are on to a road.

Turn L onto the road but then R after only about 200 metres onto the signposted bridleway (*alternative start point if you have cycled from Chesterfield station). When this hard-packed farm track forks, bear R. A slight descent is followed by a gentle climb. About 800 metres will bring you to Broomhall Farm. Continue along the track you are on, ignoring a bridleway R just after the farm. Climb to Westwick Farm then, about 200 metres past this, turn R opposite a large bungalow.

This bridleway has been re-surfaced. It descends through

a farm into a dip (where it crosses a stream) then climbs to and through a small farm yard (Frith Hall) and past a pond. Ride uphill to the next farm, The Birches, and follow the bridleway to curve 90 degrees L. The surface is now a coarse gravel.

Beyond Bagthorpe Farm the track levels out. On meeting the tarmac road opposite the Royal Oak turn L. Take the next R signposted 'Wigley' and marked as a dead-end. Follow tarmac to Wigley Hall Farm ignoring a footpath L. Just L of the farm take the narrow path into the 'bush'. Slither your way through mud and over roots on this narrow indistinct path through the vast array of brambles, bushes and trees, descending parallel to the wall on your L, and later parallel with the stream.

On reaching an oak tree where the path forks, drop steeply downhill to the L on an entertaining stretch of path to a stream. Go L, ford one stream, then up the L-hand side of another and between stone gateposts. Cross R, over this second stream to a gate. The gate marks the start of a walled lane. Follow this uphill. It curves L after only 100 metres then eventually joins a tarmac drive.

Ride up this very smooth drive past a large house (Birley Farm). After a short distance turn R opposite a pond (there may also be a ford) through a bridlegate. Follow a short section of track then stay L up a driveway to the road. Turn L onto the road then second R after only 250 metres onto Spitewinter Lane. Descend for 800 metres to where a bridleway leaves the road to the R. It is a large metal gate (sign saying 'Grange Lumb Farm') and also has a fingerpost.

Go through the gate and down the hard track, then through the gate just L of the farm. Curve L and ride down a muddy path to cross the stream which feeds Crowhole Reservoir. Climb to a gate and pass below Rose Cottage (formerly Grangewood Farm) and go L up the track/drive to the road. Go L and follow the road for about 1.2km ignoring one L and one R turn-off.

You should come to a T-junction with a bridle gate and track opposite. This is the top of Hewetts Bank. Go straight across the road through the small gate to join this track. After only about 100 metres take the R-hand fork. You now have got about 1.5km of straight descent, but it is a well-used track that can get quite churned up in wet weather. Descend until you cross the stream, than at the next bridle gate turn R onto a larger track.

This track drops down before a steep climb (you will need a good run up!) mainly on tarmac. Near the top a farm drive joins from the R. Continue up to meet the road. Turn L and descend steeply to a road T-junction. Go R then after crossing a stream, immediately L on a bridleway up into the woods.

This path, heavily lined with oak and holly, is narrow and steep but short and pleasant too. Turn R at the road. Pass some very fine houses in Horsleygate then after roughly 800 metres, beside the 'Little Orchard' house, a metal fingerpost points R. This says 'Bridleway to Millthorpe half a mile', a really fun descent that used to be like a stream but has been resurfaced. At the second small gate, you have to cross a stream before meeting the Millthorpe road. Turn L uphill (unless you first want to visit the pub in Millthorpe).

Assuming you turn L (or come back to this point after dinner), climb steeply about 800 metres up the road to Cartledge Hall where a fingerpost R says 'Footpath and Bridleway to Brindwoodgate for Barlow'. Take this bridleway R, follow the track past the farm and descend to a point where you meet a large wooden five-bar gate and a field in front of you.

Here you need to curve R to follow the narrower path. What follows is a brilliant 800 metres of winding, single-track descent twisting and turning through a tunnel of trees and bushes but watch out for horses or walkers coming uphill. Don't go too fast! Soon you meet a road. Turn L, then L again on a very sharp corner. Unfortunately it is uphill!

After about 200 metres turn R on the track marked 'Unsuitable for Motors'. Follow this uphill (ignore a footpath R) until a road where you should turn R. After about 800 metres of descent, on a sharp L-hand corner, turn R onto a bridleway (Gateland Lane). It soon becomes muddy single track, widens out and then is single track again. You will have to negotiate two gates. When the path forks take the R-hand option. Cross Dunston Brook at the bottom of the woods before climbing steeply up the tarmac road to Elm Tree Farm.

On meeting the B6051 turn L into Barlow. Turn R in front of the Pump House pub and climb up the road for about 400 metres before taking the bridleway L (just past national speed restriction signs). This overgrown but now surfaced path descends to ford Sud Brook. Climb a steep mud track and go L on tarmac until you reach a proper T-junction at Cutthorpe. Turn R here and follow the road slightly uphill for less than 800 metres passing a pub and a school.

Take the first proper road L which is the entrance to Linacre Reservoir carpark where you started your ride. Well done!

12. Chatsworth

Bakewell

B6001

A619

B6408

Edensor

River
Derwent

Chatsworth
House

Monsal Trail

Fm.

Fm.

Haddon
Hall

A6

Beeley Lodge

OUT

B6012

Beeley

Rowsley
START

Northwood

BACK

1 mile

Route Details

Distance:

19 miles/30.5km

%age off road:

74%

Time:

3 1/2 hours

Height Gain:

420m

Map:

OS 1:25 000 Explorer
OL24 White Peak (east)

Facilities:

Good cafe at Rowsley
(Cauldwell Mill), & Beeley
cafe; shops and pubs at
Bakewell, other pubs on route

Rail Access:

Nearest station Matlock 7km

Route direction

Rowsley, Bouns Corner,
Bakewell, Monsal Trail,
Manners Wood, New Piece
Wood, Chatsworth, Beeley Moor,
Northwood Carr, Copy Wood,
Rowsley.

Route Summary

This route passes through
the grounds of two famous
houses (Chatsworth House and
Haddon Hall). There are ample
opportunities for refreshments
especially in Bakewell and
Rowsley. The route can easily
be shortened or lengthened
as you please. Mostly the
landscape is rolling parkland,
limestone farmland, gritstone
moors or deciduous woodland
with plenty of hills. You will
see grouse, pheasants, sheep
and perhaps deer, as well as
wild flowers and fine views of
Derbyshire. There are gravel,
grass and soil tracks, with
some ex-railway line. Some
stretches of the route can be
soggy in wet weather.

Start in Rowsley behind Cauldwell Mill, (working flour mill) at the free carpark, SK 256657. Turn L out of the carpark and after 100 metres you will meet the A6. Opposite should be the Peacock Hotel. Cross the A6 and go up the road just L of the hotel marked as a dead-end. After 600 metres uphill on tarmac, this road becomes a bridleway; a mud and stone track which climbs a further 400 metres into woodland. Just as you enter the wood proper (Bouns Corner) there are two metal gates and several converging paths. Continue along the lowest of the tracks L. Soon there is a clearing and a track forking to the R. Ride straight on downhill.

On reaching a metal gate with a fine vista (SK 244669) there are three options; L, R or straight on. Turn L, slightly uphill. The track flattens out. As you curve gently to the R ignore the track branching off slightly uphill to your L. It is soon downhill and you will pass a farm entrance on your L. The track itself soon curves R into a field but you should go straight on, following the narrow overgrown waymarked path. To your L is Bowling Green Farm. Yes it has one! Peer over the wall and you'll see it. Presumably the inhabitants of the 14th century Haddon Hall would saunter up for a genteel game after high tea.

Go through a small gate then hug the bottom fence (metal) for three fields. You are now in the park/grounds of Haddon Hall (home of the Duke of Rutland). The hall is just below you, to your L, but is hidden from view. When you meet a tarmac track turn L. It drops steeply with sharp bends. Ignore the small fork R. Continue down towards the River Wye but look for the first bridleway R which is a waymarked wooden gate beside a larger metal gate. Go through the small gate onto the field and aim for the old ash tree. Follow the sheep paths which contour round the field just above the trees. On reaching a fence, stay this side of it but turn R, up the field. At the top of the field go through the small wooden gate and turn L onto the cinder/gravel track.

In May a dense blanket of bluebells usually covers the bank to your R. The track brings you out just by the old railway viaduct

(Coombs Viaduct). Turn L and follow the minor road into Bakewell.

You will come out at the junction between the B6408 and the A619 near the river. A stone pinnacle sits in the centre of the road. Turn R up the A road and after about 400 metres go L along Holme Lane. On your L you will soon see a packhorse bridge over the river. Go R opposite this on a bridleway (stone track) which climbs steeply through an old quarry. Go through the gate and onto fields, passing another old quarry and cow pond before a second gate leads into a stretch of walled lane. Follow this bridleway down over bumpy fields, alongside the wall until you meet the old railway (Monsal Trail).

Turn R and follow the railway for over 3km until you meet a gate across the track and a sign just in front of it which says 'End of Trail'. Leave the trail here. Drop down onto a well-surfaced track/road. Turn L, pass under the now familiar viaduct and ride uphill past Coombs Farm. You will climb steadily uphill to reach the point you were at earlier in the ride (SK 244669). This time take the steepest uphill path; the mud one, L into the woods. At the next track T-junction turn L uphill then after a short distance turn R to climb even more steeply.

Luckily this bridleway soon levels before curving R through a stone gateway. You curve immediately L. Pick your way judiciously along the muddy wooded path until a sharp R takes you over the sad remains of a stone wall to a stile and double gate. Bump or slide (depending on the season) straight down the grass field aiming roughly half way along the plantation below. The bridleway is marked by wooden posts.

You should join a mud track and come to a gate. Go through the gap in the plantation via this large gate then turn R to follow the bottom wall. You will soon come to another gate where a track bears L. Head left up this track/bridleway over a field, then go through New Piece Wood.

As you come out of the wood you should get a good view of Chatsworth House below (home of the Duke of Devonshire with famous gardens designed by Joseph Paxton). Ride downhill on grass to the first waymarking post. Fork R here just above the young trees. Follow the wide, flat grass track almost parallel to the top wall before dropping diagonally R over the grass to join the road at Lindup Low (not particularly obvious on the ground). Turn R down the road, ride over the humpback bridge then turn immediately L just above Beeley Lodge.

Head up the steep unclassified road towards the moors. There is now a steady climb of a good 2.5km. Tarmac soon gives way to a rough but dry stony farm track. On meeting the road at the top turn L. (In summer at weekends there is often an ice cream van here). Climb up the road and ignore the road which forks L. Take the first R which is approx. 1.6km from where you left Beeley Plantation.

It is a rough gravelly track opposite a road turning L. Ride along the rough potholed track until you meet the road again. Turn R and ride along the road for just less than 1.6km. There is a road L which should be ignored and then a slight rise. The road flattens out. Just before a R-hand corner and the brow of the hill turn L off the road through double wooden gates (bridleway fingerpost).

The obvious path among the sheep descends over the moor above Fallinge Edge. There are fine surrounding views. A wooded section with muddy patches follows. As the path curves R you'll see a stream to your L. The path forks. Take the higher path, R, which is narrow, reasonably flat and contours through Northwood Carr along the side of the hill for about 800 metres to a small bridle gate. This is a lovely stretch of singletrack through oak /mixed woodland.

After this gate go down the track to your L for only 20 metres to a junction of paths. You need to go through two large gates so that you cross the track in front of you and continue straight on into Copy Woods. A mud path with some bumps takes you along to a road. Go L, very steeply downhill into Rowsley.

Turn L at the bottom and then turn R onto the A6. Pass over the river before turning left to finish back at Cauldwell Mill carpark.

Above, Chatsworth House, surrounded by the Paxton Gardens

13. Middleton-by-Youlgreave

Tissington Trail

Parsley Hay

A515

(Buxton)

High Peak Trail

P

D.O.T.

Biggin

Newhaven

Kenslow Fm.

Pikehall

A5012

Long Dale

START

Middleton-by-Youlgreave

Mouldridge Grange

Gratton Dale

1 mile

Route Details

Distance:

15 miles/24km

%age off road:

80%

Time:

3 hours

Height Gain:

290m

Map:

OS 1:25 000 Explorer OL24 White Peak (east and west)

Facilities:

Pubs in M-by-Y and Biggin, tea, snacks, toilet and cycle hire at Parsley Hay

Rail Access:

No station near by

Route direction

Long Dale, Pikehall, Biggin, Tissington Trail, Parsley Hay, High Peak Trail, Middleton-by-Youlgreave.

Route Summary

This route is on hilly limestone farmland mainly in open countryside, with largely gravel surfaces or soil tracks with some grass. It also includes small sections of both the High Peak and Tissington Trails; flat disused railway lines, ideal for, and well used by, both walkers and cyclists. There are short muddy stretches in wet weather but generally surfaces are good (nothing too rough). This route could be ridden on a touring bike.

Start in Middleton-by-Youlgreave SK 195632. If you want the option, you can extend this ride by linking it to the Darley Bridge Circle which would add another 18mls/29km but bring you back to this point.

For the standard Milddleton-by-Youlgreave route, from Middleton take the road S towards Dale End and Elton. Roughly 1.2km on, after a downhill stretch, the road climbs gently. There is a sharp L-hand corner before the road reaches Smerill Grange Farm. On this corner, take the walled track (way-marked bridleway), the middle of three tracks. After about 600 metres uphill go through a gate, ride on or parallel to and then merge with, the gravel farm track. Continue to climb quite steeply. After a large metal gate with very fat tubular bars curve gently R. Follow the obvious track until another gate brings you to a large squarish field with lumps of limestone in its upper R-hand corner. These are the remains of an ancient burial mound. Follow the L-hand wall of this field to a gate onto the side of Long Dale.

Go L slightly downhill and descend diagonally into the dale. Long Dale is a small steep-sided grassy dale which is usually quiet. You will soon come to two gates. Go through the small wooden gate L rather than the large metal five-bar gate straight on. Follow Long Dale until it meets the head of Gratton Dale. At this point go through the gate and turn R. Follow the path as it climbs up and then winds round the hill to the L, passing through another gateway. Head R across to the limestone wall then follow it to the A5012.

Turn R onto the road then take the first L opposite Mouldridge Grange (signposted 'Parwich'). About 600 metres up this road, just before a R-hand bend, turn R onto the unclassified road. Ride down this walled track to Holly Bush Farm and the main road. Turn L. After 100 metres go L onto a smaller road.

You are now in Pikehall and should turn R onto the unclassified road which runs just under Cottage Farm. This well-

Route 13: Middleton-by-Youlgreave

surfaced hard track climbs uphill about 800 metres to cross the High Peak Trail (signed 'Pennine Bridleway'). Another 800 metres should bring you to a T-junction. Turn R. A km-long downhill stretch will take you to the A515 (Ashbourne to Buxton road). Go R then immediately L on a road signposted 'Biggin'. You will soon see a bridge crossing the road. On the near side of the bridge, to the R, a small path leads onto the Tissington Trail.

Turn R to follow it N. The smooth cinder surface should prove pleasant riding. After roughly 5km the High Peak Trail will intercept your route at an acute angle from the R. 800 metres on, is Parsley Hay picnic site and cycle-hire centre. If it is open you can buy sweets and drinks here. From Parsley Hay turn around and ride S (in the direction you've come from), this time taking the L fork to head down High Peak Trail signed 'Pennine Bridleway, Middleton Top'. After about 1.2km you pass some posts where a farm track crosses the trail; then on a little further you will reach a single gate. Turn L on the UC road (Green Lane) signed 'Middleton-by-Youlgreave'. This undulating hard-packed track will take you about 2.5km down to a tarmac road. At this road junction turn R towards Newhaven.

Take the first L off the road, a tarmac farm drive, after about 800 metres. It passes below Kenslow Farm and drops down through a gate signed 'Rookery Farm' then forks by a cow pond. Choose the L fork uphill. Soon this road descends steeply. Be ready for two severe L-hand bends especially the second. You will come out on a steep road above Middleton Hall. Turn R here and drop into Middleton-by-Youlgreave to finish.

MIDDLETON-BY-YOULGREAVE CIRCLE/DARLEY BRIDGE CIRCLE LINK

The Middleton-by-Youlgreave and Darley Bridge Circles overlap. So if you want to make a much longer ride you can combine both to make a large figure of eight shaped route. See the notes in the route descriptions.

David passing weathered boulders

The Head of Gratton Dale

14. Darley Bridge

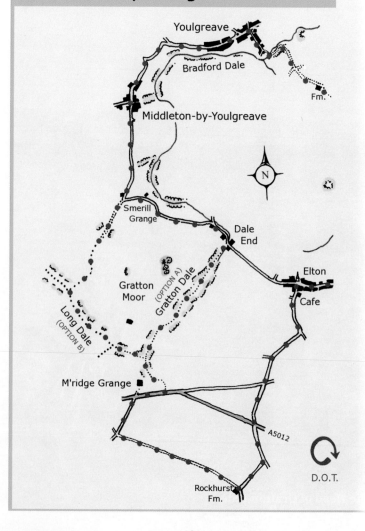

1 Mile

B5056

Birchover

Fm

Clough
Lane

Clough
Woods

→ (Winster)

Fm.

A6

START
P

WORKS

P.H.

Darley
Bridge

(Matlock)

↓

Route Details

Distance:

18 miles/29km

%age off road:

45%

Time:

3 hours

Height Gain:

490m

Map:

OS 1:25 000 Explorer OL 24
White Peak (east)

Facilities:

Shops and pubs in Youlgreave
and Birchover

Rail Access:

Nearest station Matlock 4km

Route direction

Darley Bridge, Clough
Lane, Upper Town, Elton,
Mouldridge Grange, Gratton
Dale, Middleton-by-Youlgreave,
Youlgreave, Birchover, Darley
Bridge.

Route Summary

This is a fine route using
bridleways, an old salters' lane
and stretches of unclassified
road (part of the old packhorse
routes). The landscape is a
mixture of hilly limestone
farmland and woodland, with
small quiet villages linked by
twisting roads. There are gravel
and soil tracks, some of them
rocky, with fields and limestone
dales as well. Some stretches
can be muddy in wet weather.

Start at Darley Bridge picnic site and carpark SK270623. Turn R out of the carpark onto the road. Pass the Square and Compass pub and cross the river. Take the first road R, signposted 'Enthovens', which forks after 400 metres. Take the L fork, so that as you pass the buildings and large chimneys of Enthoven's Smelting Works, all are on your R.

On entering the edge of Clough Woods the track forks. The L fork descends to Millclose Mine, once Derbyshire's largest and most prolific lead mine.You want to take the R fork which soon splits again. Ignore the lower, flatter tarmac track R. The other track, which you want, climbs steeply into the woods.

This is an old salters' lane through very pleasant mixed woodland (with plenty of wild flowers) to Upper Town. It is a loose-surfaced rocky track of about 1.6k metres length which first climbs steeply but then levels out and becomes easily rideable. Near the top of this track you go through the yard of Uppertown Farm (look out for pygmy goats and ostrich on your L) before meeting a road at a T-junction, with some restored 'stocks' opposite.

Turn L here steeply down the road which becomes very pot-holed and muddy. Take care since there are blind corners and the road is wide enough only for a car or a bike, not both! It flattens out, then climbs slightly and meets the road to Winster. Turn L onto the road and then almost immediately R onto a RUPP beside Winster Cemetery. This path is both rocky and narrow, but short and interesting.

When you meet the B5056 cross with care. Please walk up the track opposite, since the next 200 metres are on a footpath! On joining another track with a sign saying 'Limestone Way' you can re-mount. Turn R and follow it until you meet a road. Turn L onto the road which will take you to Elton.

On reaching Elton Church (to your R), go L up the road opposite, beside the Duke of York pub. Elton café (sadly to close), should be on your L. Ride less than 800 metres up the road and as it curves R ignore the road off L. You will soon reach a high point with good views. The road levels out then descends.

Go straight across the next two roads you meet. You now have to climb slightly. Again the road curves R and there is a L turn (to Aldwark) you should ignore. Further on where the road veers sharply L, turn R onto an unclassified road below Rockhurst Farm. We have known the top stretch of this track to be a foot deep in silage! Follow this stony/ gravel double-track downhill for nearly 2km until you come out on a small road.

Turn R and on meeting the A5012 go R again. Mouldridge Grange should be on your L. After 450 metres, on your L is a gate and a post marked 'Public Bridleway Gratton Dale and Long Dale'. If you want to, before finishing this ride you can extend it from here by doing the Middleton-by-Youlgreave Circle as well which should add another 15 miles/24km and rejoin this route at Middleton-by-Youlgreave. Turn L here onto the field and follow the limestone wall straight on to a corner then L. Next the bridleway cuts diagonally R across the grass field down to track through a gateway. This bumpy path curves R and down to two gates. From these gates are two options to take you to Middleton-by-Youlgreave:

A. To continue down Gratton Dale which in winter and wet conditions might involve a very muddy walk of 1.5km, or B. Go left along Long Dale which is rideable on grass.

Option A. Go through the small gate into the steep-sided rocky Gratton Dale and follow the path slightly downhill. This is a very bumpy rocky section which can be muddy and is not the place to ride your normal touring iron. Take care on any type of bike. When you come to the road at the bottom you will probably be glad you have. You are at Dale End. Turn L. Soon the road forks and you should go L up a steep but short climb. The road then descends and flattens on its way to Middleton-by-Youlgreave.

Option B. Turn L through a large wooden gate into Long Dale. It is grassy and flat. Follow this for roughly 1 km until the next bridlegate. Pass through this and turn R to follow the obvious path up the side of the dale to a large metal five-bar gate. Next follow the R-hand wall of this large field to another five-bar gate into a walled 'funnel'. Pass through another big gate then follow the bridleway downhill alongside the L-hand wall, into a walled lane down to the road. Turn L and follow the road to Middleton-by-Youlgreave to rejoin the route.

Middleton-by-Youlgreave is a pleasant small village but without a shop or pub. In mid to late May decorative well dressings can be seen here. Pass through the village (unless you'd like a pleasant walk down Bradford Dale) and when you meet a larger road turn R. Ride down the road into Youlgreave. You will pass the Farmyard Inn and then a large circular stone monument (conduit/reservoir head). Turn next R with care, on the small road just in front of the imposing stone church and drop steeply. Ignore the fork R signposted 'Unsuitable for Motors'. After 150 metres, just as the road curves R you should be able to see a small limestone crag and the river below you. On your L is 'Braemor House'. Turn L just above the house down the narrow bridleway. It is a steep gravel path with a humpback bridge and ford at the bottom. Cross the river and turn L on the tarmac track. A short way on, you should follow the road as it curves R, uphill away from the river. This bridleway continues uphill. Ignore the track which crosses yours and pass Lower Greenfields Farm on your R. You will come to another larger farm on your R. Pass through the small gate just L of the larger five-bar one. Ride straight on across the field, almost following the R-hand wall. You should come to a gate beside a large ash tree. Again go straight across the next field to join a back road (to Elton).

Cross the road, and pass through the gate opposite. Ride straight across the field, to a medium sized bridlegate. As you begin to descend more steeply curve R, passing under the small wooded area before joining the path that leads to a gate and small bridge across a stream. Ride diagonally R to join the road and turn R. A short way up this road take the first road L up to Birchover. It enters the village by the Druid Inn. From here you have two options:

Long Dale, Middleton-by-Youlgreave Route

(Option 1) Turn right in Birchover just above the Methodist chapel, onto the small road to Upper Town, then go down the salters' lane you came up at the start of the ride, back to Darley Bridge.

(Option 2) Follow the road up out of Birchover. Turn first R in front of Stanton Park Quarry (gritstone), ride down to Stanton Lees and then turn R again to Darley Bridge, all on the road. Take care as these roads are very steep and winding with blind corners.

15. Ashover

START
Eddlestow Lot

Vernon Lane

(Chesterfield)

A632

Kelstedge

P.H.

(Matlock)

Slack Hill

River Amber

Ashover

P.H.

P.H.

D.O.T.

Coffin Lane

P.H.

Milltown

1/2 mile

Route Details

Distance:

7 1/2 miles/12km

%age off road:

60%

Time:

1 1/2 hours

Height Gain:

225m

Map:

OS 1:25 000 Explorer OL 24
The Peak District, White Peak
Area or 1:50 000 Landranger
119 Buxton and Matlock

Facilities:

Pubs and shops in Ashover

Rail Access:

nearest station Matlock 9km

Route direction

Eddlestow Lot, Vernon Lane,
Kelstedge, Ashover, Abrahams
Lane, Milltown, Coffin Lane,
Eddlestow Lot.

Route Summary

This is a really enjoyable short
ride. It is varied and quite
rough in places. It has become
a favourite with many riders
and has been reproduced in
magazines and other guide
books which call it 'a Classic'.
It passes through lovely
deciduous woodlands with wild
flowers and includes several
stream crossings which can
be feisty. Many of the paths
are quite narrow and can
sometimes be overgrown. The
rock/mud/sand surfaces can
become heavy going when wet
but the majority are rideable
and fun even in winter.

Start SK 324632 at Eddlestow Lot carpark/picnic site, Wirestone Quarry (disused). Turn R out of the carpark and down the road for about 300 metres. Take the first gravel track R. This is Vernon Lane (signed Vernon Lane Farm). A short way down this track you'll come to a farm gateway with steel gates and a small millstone set into the wall. Go down the narrow path just L of the gates. Narrow with a rocky/sandy surface and steeply downhill, this path is rideable but remember horses and walkers use it too! Follow this path down through pleasant mixed woodland.

It flattens out, then comes to a ford beside a small stone bridge. Cross the stream as you see fit and follow the wider path straight on (ignore the small path L) to another ford and bridge. Again go straight on following the main path out of the woods along tarmac to meet the A632 at Kelstedge.

Turn L up the A632. Pass the Kelstedge Inn and a turn off to Ashover, both on your R, then just beyond Bungalow Farm and national speed restriction road signs, turn R down the green lane towards Marsh Green. Again it is quite a bumpy rutted path that can be muddy. Drop downhill, ride through a small ford and along the main track until you come out at a road (where a footpath goes R). Go L and up to a T-junction. Here take the road R, into Ashover.

Ride past Ashover Post Office then curve R passing the Crispin Inn and the church on your R. As you come to the next T-junction you should face The Old Poet's Corner pub. Turn L here onto Hockley Lane. Ignore the first bridleway almost immediately R. Ride down the road for about 300 metres then take the bridleway (Abrahams Lane) which leaves the road by going R opposite two small houses. It is only narrow so don't miss it! (The route drops off the edge of the White Peak map here but only for 3km) Follow Abrahams Lane down to, and then parallel with the stream. The path crosses the stream (River Amber) on a fine stone slab bridge then follows the other bank until a gate beside a farmhouse and large wooden workshop.

Pass the houses and turn L when you meet a road. Follow the tarmac downhill, initially curving R and then cross a bridge over the stream. Turn R here and then R again when you reach the Miners Arms pub. This road soon forks and you should veer R uphill.

After 200 metres the road curves sharply L and there is a quarry entrance to your R. On this corner leave the road to follow an overgrown path (unclassified road) directly ahead of you. You will climb slightly into the woods on a narrow mud and stone path. Follow it up and down for roughly 800 metres to a clearing where a wider gravel track crosses yours. Ashover should be visible down to your R and the small path in front of you is edged with stone slabs on end. Turn L onto the larger track here and follow it for 200 metres to another large gravel track.

To the L is Overton Hall. Continue along the bridleway you are on by crossing straight over the large track. Ride up the 'Coffin Lane' paved with stone slabs into the woods. After passing through the woods colonised by huge rhododendrons you will come out onto old mine spoil heaps below the gritstone Cocking Tor. Follow the same line as the path took through the woods. Ride over the spoil heaps gaining not losing height, traversing round the hill to join a muddy track which climbs more steeply towards Ravensnest.

This becomes tarmac and climbs to Red House Farm where you come to a road junction. From here on it's all road. Turn R and follow the very straight road for about 1.5km. Then it bends sharp L before joining the A632 at the top of Slack Hill. Turn L then immediately R signposted 'Beeley, Darley Dale'. The next R-hand turn leads back to your starting point.

16. Manifold

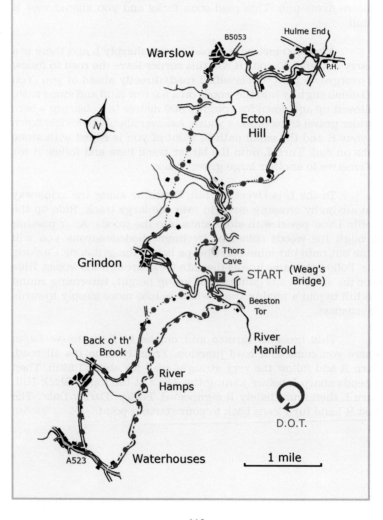

Hulme End
B5053
Warslow
Ecton
Hill
P.H.
N
Thors
Cave
Grindon
START
(Weag's
Bridge)
P
Beeston
Tor
River
Manifold
Back o' th'
Brook
River
Hamps
D.O.T.
A523
Waterhouses
1 mile

Route Details

Distance:

18 miles/29km

%age off road:

72%

Time:

4 1/2 hours

Height Gain:

390m

Map:

OS 1:25 000 Explorer OL24 White Peak (west)

Facilities:

Tea rooms/snacks at Wetton Mill SK096561, Lea House SK094516, two cycle hire centres and pub at Warslow and Hulme End. Cafes, shops and pubs at Hartington.

Rail Access:

No station nearby

Route direction

Weag's Bridge, Manifold Light Railway, Waterhouses, Waterfall, Grindon, Warslow, Hulme End, Back of Ecton, Light Railway, Weag's Bridge.

Route Summary

Straddling the Derbyshire/Staffordshire border this route explores the heavily wooded and dramatic Manifold valley and some of the surrounding limestone upland dotted with sheep farms. The track of the Manifold Light Railway closed in 1934 forms part of the route. There are dramatic views, caves with evidence of early man, rock outcrops, and a river that vanishes down swallow holes in the summer. In mid summer the trees and rich meadows full of grasses and wild flowers are great.

At least half of the route is easy riding and fairly flat using cycle tracks and small roads but the other half is steeply up and down with grassy and bumpy stretches which need some walking here and there even in dry weather (no more than 1.5km walking in the whole route). The route passes within half a mile of Wetton Mill with its mediaeval farm, café and campsite.

In winter the stretch between Grindon and Warslow will have some very muddy sections.

Start in the carpark lay-by near Weag's Bridge SK 100541 (a bridge here was shown on maps dated 1737). Standing with your back to the river turn L out of the lay-by, cross the small road (but not the river), and go through the gateway onto the R of the two tarmac tracks in front of you. This is the Manifold Way, which used to be a Light Railway. At first you will ride alongside the River Manifold but then you curve R (the large crag above you to the left is Beeston Tor) and wind along, crossing back and forth over the river Hamps. After following this flat track for about 5km you will meet the A523 at Waterhouses.

At the A523 cross the fast road with care. Turn R onto a cycle track. Cycle along this track and then the road for nearly 800 metres before taking the first R turn opposite Ye Olde Crown Hotel. Cross the river on a humpback bridge and follow this road. You will curve R then begin to climb uphill. Roughly 1.2km should bring you to a junction. Continue straight on but take the next R turn after only 100 metres. This road sweeps downhill and through a ford to Back o'th'Brook. After the ford curve R up the road with a dead-end sign. It traverses up and round the hill for a good 800 metres before reaching a large gate and bridlegate beside it.

Go through this and up the track to the farm, where two more gates take you through the yard. Watch out for a goose! Next go through the metal five-bar gate in front of you before dropping down the field on the track slightly to the L. You should aim to go through the metal gate into the L-shaped field with the cow pond in it. Follow the grass track uphill to the R where there is a gateway at the highest point of the field. From the gateway go straight ahead so you cut off the R-hand corner of the field but rejoin the R-hand wall by hawthorn trees.

Now follow this R-hand edge, through one bridle gate, across another field and then through a second gate. Keep following this edge for the next field too, until you reach a slightly larger gate in the corner. Go through the gate and then drop diagonally down the grass field aiming just L of the stone barn. As you approach the corner of the field wall attached to the barn, curve R round it through a gate. Drop down the bank to the bridlegate and up the steep field following the R-hand wall. Keep close to the R-hand wall. After two gateways you meet a very steep road. If you want to cut the ride short here, turn R down the road. It is less than 400 metres to your starting point. To continue the ride turn L steeply uphill to Grindon. On the road into the village take the first fork R, to pass a row of terraced houses.

At the church the road curves sharp L. Turn R immediately above the play area, down the road with a dead-end sign. The road dips, down then up, then descends again for 300 or 400 metres. Where the tarmac becomes a stone track, at a large field before the farm buildings, look for a bridle gate and stile on your L.

From here to Warslow is a stretch over grass fields which involves losing and gaining height several times. There are muddy patches and some walking will be needed.

Go through the gate, diagonally across the field, through a large gate and down the next field to a line of ash and hawthorn. After a small gate ride down the L-hand edge of the field to another gate. Follow the damp, rocky path downhill to cross Hoo Brook on a small concrete and metal foot bridge (ignore the wooden bridge L). After 20 metres there is a bridlegate and then a small wooden bridge. Negotiate these then turn immediately L on the steeply uphill grass bridleway following the L-hand edge of the field.

Continue in this manner over the next three fields negotiating gates as necessary. At the road go straight across through the gate, and down two fields to a farm track. Cross this too, go through the large metal five bar gate and down two fields with gates to a long narrow field.

Cross diagonally over this, and the next field to cross a stream, go through a small gate and start climbing. Follow the R-hand hedge to the gate. Go straight across the next field to a gate and then follow a stretch of gravelly track to a road. Cross the road and go through the bridle gate opposite into a steep rocky, tree-lined walled lane. Some parts may be very difficult to pass. At the bottom ford the stream (wet feet?), then walk uphill to the bridlegate in the R-hand corner. Another walled stretch and gate bring you to a gravel track in front of houses. Curve R until you meet tarmac then bear L up the road into Warslow.

On meeting the B5053 turn R. Ignore the road off L unless you want to visit the Greyhound pub (welcoming with home-cooked food) but take the next turn R, signposted 'Ecton and Manifold Valley'. Go first R again, down a fine hill, cross the River Manifold and then turn L onto the old Light Railway.

Follow this to the B5054 at Hulme End. Turn R, then next R signposted 'Wetton and Alstonfield'. Take the next R again, then the first L signposted 'Back of Ecton, No Through Road'. After roughly 1.5km at Back of Ecton, you should come to a hairpin corner (steeply uphill) where a road forks off L. Take this L downhill, past Lees Farm, to Manor House. Go through the large wooden gate beside a stream, and follow the stream (which may dry to a trickle in summer) all the way down a lovely small grassy limestone dale. At the bottom cross the road, then the river, back onto the light railway track. Follow this for about 1.5km due S back to your starting point.

Opposite: Thor's Cave

17. Derby North

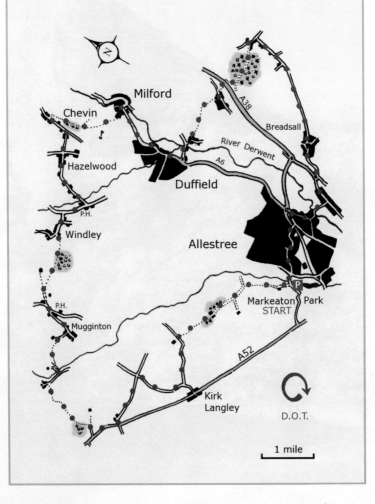

Milford

Chevin

Hazelwood

P.H.

Windley

P.H.

Mugginton

A38

Breadsall

River Derwent

A6

Duffield

Allestree

P
Markeaton Park
START

A52

Kirk
Langley

D.O.T.

1 mile

Route Details

Distance:

25 miles/40km

%age off road:

40%

Time:

5 hours

Height Gain:

530m

Map:

OS 1:25 000 Explorer 259 Derby

Facilities:

Shops and pubs on route

Rail Access:

Derby station 3.5km

Route direction

Markeaton, Mercaston, Muggington, Windley, Hazelwood, Chevin, Milford, Duffield, Brackeley Gate, Breadsall, Markeaton.

Route Summary

Derby North Circle links up some interesting sections of off-road cycling north of Derby. Doing this does involve a fair amount of road work. However the roads used are generally quiet country lanes. Keep an eye out for hedge cuttings and do not forget to take your spare inner tube and puncture repair kit.

Start at Mundy Play Centre car park, north of Markeaton Park SK 332380. Heading N out of the car park turn R then immediately L onto a track to Markeaton Stones. Follow this obvious track for roughly 800 metres until a T-junction with a tarmac road. Turn L uphill. Choose the R fork to Upper Vicarwood Farm. Here you need to pass through a large gate to continue along the bridleway just below the brick stables. Follow the track round the field's edge to a road.

Turn L onto Lodge Lane. After about 1.2km go R towards Mercaston. Ride along Flagshaw Lane for roughly 1.5km to a cross roads. Take a L turn and cycle to the Ashbourne road (A52). Turn R towards Brailsford. You need the next R after roughly 800 metres and just by a 30mph countdown sign. Don't miss it.

Ride along this track until, just before a cattle grid, there is a L turn. Take this and leave the tarmac behind. This takes you along Woods Lane (track), which after a good 1.5km rejoins tarmac just outside Mercaston. Turn R onto the road. After 500 metres go L on the track signposted 'Bridleway to Muggington'.

After only 200 metres leave the large track by turning R. Ride very briefly along a shallow stream to a path which leads to a bridlegate. From here ride uphill following the L edge of the next two fields. Descend to a gate. Turn R onto Hunger Lane which climbs to Muggington.

Take a L turn. Ride 800 metres to a road junction (rear of The Cock Inn). Go L but after only 200 metres, turn R. Ride down this track passing through a number of gates until you come to two large metal gates side by side.

Go through the L-hand gate and follow the R edge of the field to a bridlegate. Go through this, then ride across to and through another gate. Head up to the top of the hill riding parallel to the edge of the woods. Ride down the track which follows the wood's edge.

When you reach two five bar gates take the R-hand gate (Amber Valley routeway No.2) to cross a field diagonally on a rough track. Continue down this track until, where the track bends sharp L you reach a small bridlegate. Go through the bridlegate then bear L keeping the farm buildings (Chapel Farm) to your R. A gate takes you out onto the road opposite Windley Baptist Chapel.

From here turn right to follow Windley Lane nearly 800 metres to the Wirksworth road. Turn R here. Take the next L onto Nether Lane which climbs just over 1.5km to Hazlewood crossroads. Go straight on. Take the next L towards Farnah Green.

As you ride downhill, after 500 metres, you should see the Bluebell Inn on your L. Take the signposted bridleway R just after the Bluebell. This is North Lane, a fine sandy track about 2.5km which takes you S over the top of the Chevin on the line of a prehistoric ridgeway. Watch out for low flying golf balls!

Descend into Milford. At the bottom, by the Strutt Arms, turn R onto the A6 and follow it for about 1.5km into Duffield. Go past the shops then take the first proper road L (Makeney Road). You will cross the River Derwent, then turn immediately R past the Bridge Inn. Continue up this hill 200 metres to Eaton Bank. Here just before the road levels, take the signposted bridleway back L. At the end of the short lane the bridleway heads uphill behind the house. You may have to get off and shoulder your bike on the next bit which has steps, but you can soon remount. Ride across to a bridlegate.

Stick to the R-hand side of the field and pass through a number of gates for roughly 800 metres. The final gate should take you into Eaton Park woods. Follow the path downhill through this pleasant woodland to come out on Alfreton Road.

Turn L and pass the Bell and Harp pub. There is a bridleway sign just before the national speed limit sign. Turn R down Toad Lane.

Go over a level crossing, over Bottle Brook, straight across Derby Road and under the A38 to a gate. At this point ride L up the field's edge. Go through a gate and turn L onto the lane. Ride steadily uphill on this good sandy track for about 1.6km through woodland (Horsley Carr). Ignore tracks off to the L and R. You should come out at Brackley Gate.

Turn R, then R again along Quarry Road which leads straight along the line of Ryknild Street to Breadsall. This becomes Moor Road as you enter Breadsall. Pass the stone church on your L then turn R. Continue until you meet a T-junction. Turn R on Croft Lane signposted 'Derby'.

From here on, back through Derby, you have to cross some very busy roads so take extra care. Follow Croft Lane to a large roundabout. Go straight across following signs to Alfreton Road Industrial Estate. After roughly 800 metres take the first R turn, Haslams Lane towards the Rugby Club. This leads to Darley Abbey Industrial Estate. Go through the estate crossing the River Derwent via a Toll Bridge. Cycle up Old Lane to a T-junction where you should turn R onto Church Lane. Continue uphill until you meet Duffield Road (A6). Go L, then after only 400 metres, R up Ferrers Way. Follow this for about 800 metres until you meet a T-junction with Birchover Way where you should turn L.

Ride downhill to a road junction. Turn L onto Kedleston Road then immediately R down Markeaton Lane. A short way along this lane on your L is Mundy Play Centre where you started your ride.

Opposite: Descending on the Chevin. A classic mix of roots and gritstone steps

18. Ashbourne

Route Details

Distance:

19.5 miles/31.5km

%age off road:

48%

Time:

4 1/2 hours

Height Gain:

510m

Map:

OS 1:25 000 Explorer maps OL24 White Peak and 259 Derby (split between two maps!) or whole route on 1:50 000 Landranger 119 Buxton and Matlock

Facilities:

Pubs, shops, cafes and cycle hire in Ashbourne, tea kiosk at Tissington and in summer cream teas at Bassat Wood Farm, near Tissington SK 177512

Rail Access:

Rail Access: nearest station Cromford 11km if you join the route at Kniveton.

Route direction

Ashbourne, Tissington Trail, Tissington Ford, Kniveton, Atlow, Ridge Lane, Moorend, Osmaston Park, Wyaston, Ashbourne.

Route Summary

This route has mixed terrain and surfaces including a fair amount of old railway cinder track and pleasant small roads. It is also suitable, especially in dry weather, for the reasonably adventurous touring bike rider if you don't mind a little walking. Likely muddy spots are: the far end of Osmaston Park and Wigber Low. There are some fine views of Carsington Water and limestone farmland, and down towards Derby if you are blessed with clear weather.

Start in Ashbourne at the Leisure Centre car park SK 178463 or at the Tissington Trail cycle hire centre at Ashbourne SK 175469. There is a long tunnel, with cycle trail that takes you from the Leisure Centre to the cycle hire centre. Ride N along this flat disused railway for 5.5km until the picnic site and car park at Tissington (tea/snacks shop). Leave the trail here. The scenic village of Tissington is along the small road to your L. To continue the ride you need to turn R towards Bradbourne. Ignore the R turn to Basset Wood Farm (unless you need a cream tea break) and cycle a mile along this unfenced road before dropping very steeply to cross a brook via a slippery ford or bridge.

20 metres on turn R before the cattle grid, cross the B5056 on the new crossing. Ride only 25m uphill, then turn R onto the muddy track and ride diagonally uphill. At the top of the hill, in the field, do not follow the R-hand wall as the track appears to, but go across to a metal bridlegate (L/H corner of the field) onto a walled path. Come out of the walled path through a small wooden gate. Go straight on through the next large gate and then follow the R-hand wall while contouring round Wigber Low. Go through the next gateway then curve slightly L. Soon you will see Longrose Farm and large barns (with corrugated roofs) ahead of you. You reach a large five-bar gate. Pass through this into the field in front of Longrose Farm. Beware, I got chased by about a dozen bullocks here! If you have similar problems shout loudly at them. Ride straight across the field to a footpath stile opposite. Do not go through it but follow the hedge down to join a grassy hedged track. Pass top side of the riding stables through a narrow gap. Ride up their drive to meet a small road.

Turn R then after 250 metres turn first L through a large metal gate onto a small road/track. You should soon reach a larger road, the B5035 from Middleton. Go almost straight across and up the track opposite signposted 'Unsuitable For Motors'. Follow this track on a tarmac surface at first, for roughly 350 metres. It curves R and forks. Take the L fork on the track marked Atlow Winn farm. On your L you should get good views of Carsington

Reservoir. Ride along, then downhill slightly, until you curve R and see a number of corrugated metal cow/sheep barns on your L. Here go through a large metal gate straight ahead onto a field. There is a fun descent down this field running parallel to but roughly 50 metres away from the L-hand hedge line. You will reach another large gate opposite a stone barn and should pass through it and turn L onto tarmac.

Descend to cross the stream (Henmore Brook) in Atlow before going R at the grass triangle signed Bradley, Biggin and Kirk Ireton. After less than 800 metres' climb, at the next road junction turn R signed Bradley and Ashbourne then immediately R again on a vehicle-width track (Ridge Lane) which you should follow for the next 2km. It goes to a gate, down a field into a wooded area, stay L and follow this side of the stream out to meet a small tarmac road.

Turn L and ride the short climb to the A517 Ashbourne road. Go straight across with great care (you are in a dip, hidden from cars, on a very fast road) following the sign marked 'Moorend, Ednaston'. Follow this road through 'Hole in the Wall', a building with an archway over the road.

Ignore the L turn (Hadly Lane). After about 400 metres the road curves sharply L (ignore Osmaston fork to your R). A further 700 metres should bring you to a cross-roads with a small triangle of grass. Turn R here onto Rough Lane. After 300 metres you will come to a building. Follow the road as it bends 90 degrees L. A pleasant gated section of road takes you to the A52. Go L then next R signposted 'Shirley'.

As soon as you pass the village sign turn R (dead-end sign). Follow this road for roughly 800 metres to a large gate. This bridleway becomes a gravel, then mud track which soon drops into Osmaston Park where a lake and water-wheel make a very pleasant spot to stop for a snack. After replenishment follow the bridleway straight up from the pond, ignoring the track R after 200 metres.

At Osmaston (thatched cottages) go L and straight back into the park on the main tree-lined drive (bridleway to Wyaston).

This soon forks R, then bends and goes over a cattle grid. At the T-junction turn R and follow the waymarked gravel track down and up a large dip, through a gate (the L of the two) and down to some woods, passing a gravel parking spot. Go through two more wooden gates then up a grass field. Join the muddy, hedged track to Wyaston Grange.

On meeting the road turn R, then R again after 600 metres. The second road L, about 500 metres beyond the Shirehorse Inn should be Wyaston Road which you need to follow until Ashbourne. You will meet a dead-end sign at the top of a steep hill. Go R to follow the one-way system and signs to Ashbourne centre.

In Ashbourne, at the five-way junction with traffic lights, turn L onto the A515. Take the first R after only 300 metres then L to the Leisure Centre where you started.

Opposite: the author choosing the ford over the bridge at Ashover

19. Doveridge

N

Fm.
Abbots-
holme Sch.

Sedsall
Fm.

Fm.

Wadley

River Dove

Farm

Farm

Farm

Shooting
Club

Marston Lane

START

Doveridge

A50 (T)

D.O.T.

1 mile

Route Details

Distance:

8 miles/13km

%age off road:

50%

Time:

2 hours

Height Gain:

190m

Map:

OS 1:50 000 Landranger 128
Derby

Facilities:

Pub at Doveridge

Rail Access:

Nearest station Uttoxeter 3km

Route direction

Doveridge, Eaton Hall Farm,
Abbotsholme School, Waldley,
Marston, Woodhouse Farm,
Marston Lane, Doveridge.

Route Summary

A circuit through the rolling
farmland on the Derbyshire/
Staffordshire border, skirting
the plain of the River Dove
which forms the county
boundary. Beginning and
ending in Doveridge, it is a
rich, subtle landscape of red-
brick farms, open fields and
wooded hill slopes. You will
see the massive JCB Plant
near Rocester, and in contrast,
several impressive country
houses. The riding is on a
mixture of muddy tracks and
small tarmac roads.

Start in Doveridge. Parking is available in the cul-de-sac just past the Cavendish Arms, SK 116343. Pedal along Upswood Road, crossing the A50(T) by a bridge. When this road forks bear L. A good 800 metres will take you to where the tarmac ends and you head down towards Doveridge Clay Sports Club. Pass the Club House, then take the track to the L, to pass below the farm buildings. Carry straight on.

About 800 metres further on, this good track over fields will bring you to a junction and four-way fingerpost. Turn R on the bridleway towards a brick farm, signposted bridle road to Sedsall and Abbotsholme. The track curves L below Eaton Dovedale Farm, but leads along to a splendid uninhabited brick farm, Sedsall Farm.

From here bear L on the track just below the farmhouse, signposted 'Staffs. Way'. This bridleway passes through a gate then after 250 metres through another. The bridleway should leave the footpath here. However on the ground it is difficult to follow the line of the bridleway as shown on the OS map. Instead you will have to walk the Staffs. Way footpath for the next 400 metres. To do this go straight down the field, pass through the gate and curve R.

Follow this path along side the River Dove until you come to a small footbridge over a stream. Do not cross the bridge but cross an even smaller stream straight ahead into Staffordshire where the line of the bridleway becomes footpath, so please walk the next section.

Pass through a rusty gate and up a narrow path. You soon come out in an open field. Head straight across the field towards the farm. You should go through the large gate just R of Monk's Clownholm Farm, onto a hard track to Abbotsholme School.

You can now remount. Ride straight on, past the school

and along the drive towards to the road. Turn R and after nearly 800 metres take the first R towards Waldley and Doveridge. At the next junction turn L towards Waldley and Marston.

After 500 metres immediately after crossing Marston Brook, the road curves L but you should leave it by going through the large gate in front of you and heading up the field. Follow the L-hand edge of the field climbing to a bridle gate in the top corner. Pass through the gate and follow the R-hand edge of the field to a larger gate (the one straight in front, not on your R), go through this and follow the line of hawthorns until it curves sharp R. At this point head straight on to Banktop Farm. Go through another gate and turn R on the road.

After 400 metres this road curves L. Leave the road by forking R towards Woodhouse Farm. Pass the first farm and ride along the track. At the cattle grid do not go down between the farm buildings but take the track R to follow the R-hand hawthorn hedge.

Descend this track, curving L then R. Go through the next gate and straight across to the far corner of the field where there is a stream. Ignore the gate to the L of the corner and find the small footbridge and bridle gate leading into a hedged track. At the top of the track turn L onto Marston Lane. After crossing the A50(T) take a R turn just before a bus stop to follow the old line of Marston Lane to appear opposite the Cavendish Arms.

20. Ticknall/Robin Wood

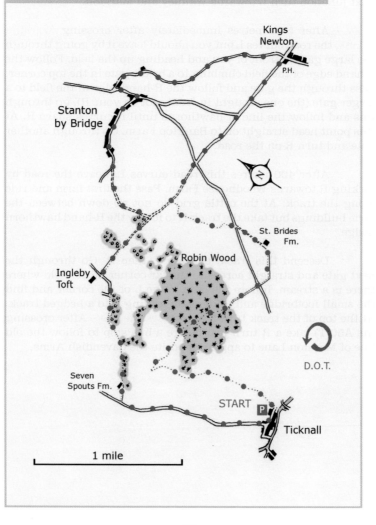

Kings Newton

P.H.

Stanton by Bridge

N

St. Brides Fm.

Robin Wood

Ingleby Toft

D.O.T.

Seven Spouts Fm.

START

P

Ticknall

1 mile

Route Details

Distance:

9.5 miles/15km

%age off road:

64%

Time:

3 hours

Height Gain:

180m

Map:

O.S. 1:25 000 Explorer 245
The National Forest

Facilities:

Pubs/shop at Ticknall, pub
at Kings Newton

Rail Access:

Burton on Trent station
9.5km if you join the route
at Seven Spouts Farm

Route direction

Ticknall, Robin Wood, Kings
Newton, Stanton by Bridge,
Ingleby Toft, Seven Spouts
Farm, Ticknall.

Route Summary

This is the most southerly of
the routes. It passes through
arable farmland and woodland
(some established and some
newly planted), bounded by the
flood plain of the Trent in the
North and the Leicestershire
boundary in the South. This
route makes a lovely afternoon
or evening ride, with tracks
mainly of gravel, sand and
mud. Some tracks over
ploughed land can be heavy
going in wet weather. There are
some fine estates and houses
(Calke Abbey is worth a visit)
as well as some traditional
farmhouses along the way.

Start in the public car park at Ticknall Village Hall on Ingleby Lane SK352240. Turn R out of the car park and take the next L, Chapel Street. Ride about 200 metres along the tarmac to meet a large gate. Go through the gap beside the gate onto the grassed area, then turn immediately L through the bridle gate onto a field.

Follow the well-marked bridleway across two fields, through Stanton Wood (a newly planted part of the National Forest 1999), across another field before cutting the corner of a field to Robin Wood (now a felled area, mainly, tree stumps). After this felled area go straight across the next field.

On reaching a hedge with a stile in it, turn R. Follow this track, at first alongside the hedge then curving L through a gap in it. This takes you into another field. Cut the R-hand corner of the field and re-enter Robin Wood through a small bridle gate. Go straight on through the woods on the wide but muddy track. When you meet a large gravel 'forestry-type' track do not turn L but join in and go straight on. Another bridle gate will take you out of the woods onto a well-surfaced track. Four hundred metres along this you will meet a road.

Cross directly over it into the field opposite. Ride along the field boundary, which soon curves sharply L down to St. Bride's Farm. Turn L to follow the now gravel and tarmac track above the farm buildings back to the road. Cross the road again onto the bridleway opposite. This bridleway, a sandy track with some puddles, is quite well defined on the ground. It crosses four fields then comes to a T-junction with a tarmac drive. At the T-junction go R and follow the tarmac for 500 metres to a crossroads. Cross the road and ride down Breach Lane opposite.

You will meet the B587 (Derby Road) in less than 800 metres. Turn R (technically straight on). After only 200 metres, when the road curves sharply R, go straight on following the signs 'Kings Newton, Isley Walton and E. Midlands Airport'. Less than

800 metres along this road you will enter the village of King's Newton and should take the track L opposite Ye Olde Packhorse Inn, signposted 'Holywell'. Follow this track for roughly 1.5km, ignoring all turnoffs. You will come to the road at Stanton by Bridge. Turn L, then first R after only 200 metres. (Alternative Start/Finish point A. SK373272). Ride up this road for about 800 metres. Once past all the houses the road soon curves sharply R and a wide farm track (unclassified road) forks L. Take the farm track and pass under the large electricity power lines. Two hundred metres more of this well-surfaced track will take you to a T-junction with another track. Turn R, past Woodhead Cottages and descend on the muddy bridleway before climbing to a small road by Ingleby Toft.

At the road turn L After only 300 metres, when the road curves sharply R leave the tarmac by riding straight on through a gap onto the narrow bridleway towards Seven Spouts Farm. Follow the wood's edge ignoring several tracks that break off L. Pass a pond; don't go L. At the farm go L up the tarmac drive. This drive winds round to meet the road. Cut the corner by leaving the drive at the first sharp R bend and pass through the gap onto the same road. Turn L and ride nearly 1.5km on tarmac to finish back in Ticknall.

Starting either of the two Ticknall routes (other starts p. 142) from Derby.

You can join either of the routes at several points by riding from Derby on the cycle way. For details see either the Sustrans or Derbyshire County Council Website.

21. Ticknall/Repton Shrubs

START
Ticknall

Saw Mills

Foremark
Reservoir

B5006

A514

Repton
Shrubs

Hartshorne

Bretby
Park

P.H.

D.O.T.

Bretby
Hall

1 mile

Route Details

Distance:

14 miles/22km

%age off road:

50%

Time:

3 hours

Height Gain:

174m

Map:

OS. 1:25 000 Explorer 245
The National Forest

Facilities:

Pubs/shop at Ticknall, pub
at Harsthorne

Rail Access:

Burton on Trent station 4km
if you join the route at Bretby

Route direction

Ticknall, Saw Mill (Milton),
Repton Common, Repton
Shrubs, Bretby, Bretby Hall,
Hartshorne, Ticknall.

Route Summary

This is a great route for a
summer evening or half day
ride. It is all rideable and is not
technical or difficult although
patches are muddy and can
be heavy going if very wet.
This route in the SW corner of
Derbyshire skirts the historic
town of Repton and passes
Foremark Reservoir. It gives
a good flavour of rich farming
country, with young woods of
the new National Forest, open
parkland, hedges and small
well-established woods. The
tracks are a mixture of sand
and mud. It is best ridden in the
spring.

Start SK353240, the public car park at Ticknall Village Hall on Ingleby Lane. Turn R out of the car park and down to the main street. Turn R along the A514 and take the R turn signposted 'Foremark, Errwood Reservoir'. On the first L-hand corner take a track, which leaves the road on the R (next to the cricket ground). This bridleway is not waymarked. After 40 metres, curve L following the hedge. Follow the L-hand edge of the next five fields, passing through gates as necessary. This bridleway is very much a field edge path.

You should come to a small wooden bridle gate. This takes you onto the sixth field. Follow the R-hand hedge straight on to join a larger track. Along this track is a junction with a track forking L. Ignore the track L and ride straight on, to pass under the large overhead power lines. You will soon reach the entrance to a small wood.

Ride down through the wood and out at the bottom. Follow the L edge of the next field round to a large gate, then into a hedged track. Descend this vehicle-rutted track into an open farmyard (Saw Mills); go through a gateway and up to a road. Turn L and follow this road for 1.2km (ignoring the road R to Lawn Bridge) until a sandy, well-drained track with a dead-end sign leaves the road to the R. Take this track, pass Brookdale Farm, go through a bridlegate and climb steadily.

The area to your L is Repton Common. You will soon get a good view of Foremark Reservoir. On reaching the large gate at the top of the track go through the gap beside it and turn R onto tarmac. Waste Farm is to your L.

After only 200 metres turn sharp R again, on a track down the edge of a plantation (Repton Shrubs). This fun descent for 800 metres drops you to the bottom corner of the wood. Go L, almost doubling back on yourself. As you enter the wood you will meet another track but stay on the bridleway closest to the fields on your R. Do not take any tracks deeper into the wood. Your track will probably be muddy but there is soon a good downhill section.

At the large oak tree (just before the stream), turn 90 degrees L up the path that soon passes immediately below Cherry Tree Cottage. Ride down the drive to join the road. Turn R then almost immediately L up a farm track to a large gate. Here go R through a bridlegate onto grass. Head up the field, pass just below the three large trees and join a narrow rather indistinct path that contours then climbs gently to a bridlegate.

Go through this, ride down through the woods to a curly metal bridlegate. Turn R here to join the road then go L up to Bretby. (possible alternative start point: closest point to Burton railway station).

The road curves L. Take the next L, then drive to the old Bretby Hall Hospital, now Cedar Court Nursing Home. At the main building and car park turn L. Go R just before the large ornamental gates. Descend the well-compacted track, pass between two ponds and ride straight on uphill. At the brow you will cross what appears to be some kind of horse race track before slithering down a muddy track into Hoofies Wood. At the bottom turn R, ride along past Hoofies Farm and through a metal gate into the field.

Now head downhill, slightly to the L and pass through the large gate. Follow the L edge of the field. Ride down the path, cross the stream, then up a short climb to the road and turn R. In Hartshorne turn L opposite the Chesterfield pub up Brook Street. Climb steadily on road for 800 metres. At the hilltop on a sharp L-hand bend turn R onto a track.

Follow this firm but bumpy surfaced for 800 metres, pass 'The Buildings Farm' and reach a road junction. Go straight across, up the road (Coal Lane) opposite. Take the next L signed 'Derby and Ticknall'. This is the B5006 road. Follow it back to your starting point at Ticknall!

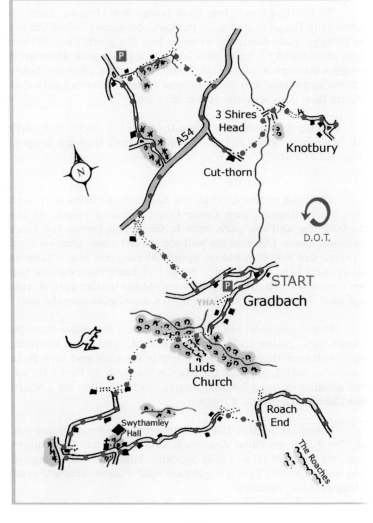

3 Shires
Head

A54

Knotbury

Cut-thorn

N

D.O.T.

START

YHA

Gradbach

Luds
Church

Swythamley
Hall

Roach
End

The Roaches

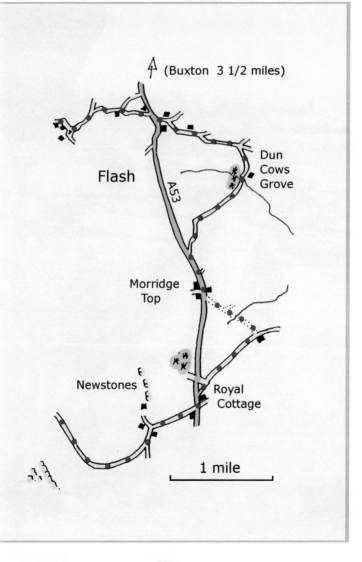

(Buxton 3 1/2 miles)

Dun Cows Grove

Flash

A53

Morridge Top

Newstones

Royal Cottage

1 mile

147

Carsington on a crisp winters day

Route Details

Distance:

23miles/36.8km

%age off road:

44%

Time:

4 hours

Height Gain:

760m

Map:

OS 1:25 000 Explorer OL24 White Peak (west)

Facilities:

Pub at Royal Cottages, pub/shop at Flash

Rail Access:

No stations nearby

Route direction

Gradbach, Lud's Church, Danebridge, Hilly Lees, Roach End, Hazel Barrow, Dun Cows Grove, Flash Bar, Knotbury, Three Shires Head, Danethorn Hollow, Wildboarclough, Tagsclough Hill, Gradbach.

Route Summary

This is a gritstone-flavoured route with high moorlands, sandy tracks and fine views based around the crags and rocky outcrops of the Roaches. It is unashamedly hilly as it dips and climbs in and out of various cloughs with many tributaries to the River Dane. Although there is a fair amount of road riding, traffic is generally very light on most stretches and it is well worth while, as you stray from Derbyshire into Staffordshire and Cheshire too. Passing through the small mixed woodlands watch out for lurking wallabies!

Start at the Peak National car park at Gradbach SK 999662. Leave the car park by turning R and follow the tarmac road, ignoring the R fork to Gradbach Youth Hostel. You will climb slightly to a cluster of houses (Gradbach itself). Continue on the obvious track as tarmac gives way to a sand and stone surface, ignoring any turn offs. This walled track drops into Gradbach Wood to a large gate with a concessionary bridleway sign and white arrow. Pass through the smaller gate to ford Black Brook and bear R uphill towards Lud's Church, signed 'Swythamley'. Follow this pleasant path with a very rideable sand and pine-needle surface through oak, pine and birch woodland to a clearing beside a small gritstone outcrop.

The footpath L leads to Lud's Church. You should leave your bike locked here and walk up to this small dramatic gorge, thought to be one of the settings mentioned in 'Gawain and the Green Knight'.

From the clearing continue straight on, out of the woodland and across moorland with bilberry and heather, then through a large gate, downhill to a fingerpost and second gate. You will be able to see the ridges of the Roaches to your L. Continue through the gate (signed 'bridleway' and 'Danebridge'). Keep on the track above the farm until a junction. Take the track downhill, leaving the prominent Hanging Stone behind you. This soon curves 90 degrees R then becomes tarmac at Park House (with a large outside wall lamp). Ride straight on to the T-junction opposite West Lodge. Turn R, then after 40 metres turn L at a second T-junction. Ignore a road that falls off to the R and curve L on the flat 'parkland' road. Pass a stone church and ride over a bridge then turn immediately L past Hillylees Farm.

This little-used road is lined with mature oak, sycamore and lime trees. It climbs steadily for a good mile towards the Roaches.

After passing a farm you will reach two large gates where

a track curves sharp L. One gate says 'Private, No Public Access'. You want the other gate on the R (finger post 'Roach End'). It leads into a field on an indistinct grass track (an unclassified road, no longer walled on the L as the map shows). It is flat and stays close to the R-hand wall until a boggy patch and a gate. Go through this, continue on until you meet tarmac and turn sharp L uphill until the 407m spot height where you should get great views.

Stay on this road as it contours round below the Roaches then swoops down and round to the L (ignore a road from the R) to a T-junction. Turn R. At the A53 turn L then R again after only 200 metres signed 'Longnor'. After cycling a good 800 metres take the track L opposite the houses (Ridge Head). This hard track soon crosses a brook which could cause large muddy patches in winter. Keep L at the track junction then R on meeting the A53.

After less than 800 metres on this busy road take the second R marked 'Unsuitable for Heavy Goods Vehicles'. A great downhill drops you into Dun Cow's Grove but a steep climb follows to a junction. Turn L. It is uphill to meet the A53 again at Flash Bar Stores. There is a pub here too if you need sustenance.

Flash claims to be England's highest village, standing at just over 1500 feet (457m). It sits just below Axe Edge (the long gritstone escarpment that the busy A53 runs along) and Axe Moor, a high exposed place which gets over 1.2 metres of rain a year and is the source of five rivers; the Dove, Manifold, Wye, Goyt and Dane (that's some sponge!).

Turn R then immediately L. Ride downhill for roughly 1.2km until a road junction with a large grass triangle. Go R here uphill on the road marked 'Dead End Except for Access'. Follow the tarmac until its demise, at a large gate. Drop 90 degrees L on a stony walled track until a gate and impressive small stone bridge over a stream. Cross the bridge and head L on a tricky rocky stretch, rideable only with care, through the next gate to come out at Three Shires Head.

This is a beautiful little spot with two packhorse bridges where two streams meet to form the River Dane. The streams form the borders of Derbyshire, Staffordshire and Cheshire. On a hot day a waterfall and the Pannier pool make a good paddling and picnic spot. Until the end of the nineteenth century this spot attracted all sorts of rogues who would cross back and forward between counties to avoid the authorities.

Pass straight across the bridge and bear L on the slightly difficult track which climbs up and round to meet a road at Cut Thorn. Turn R and continue uphill to the A54. Go R again but after less than 800 metres turn L opposite the start of the crash barriers on a track marked 'No cars except for access'. After the gate this enjoyable bit of track soon descends, curving sharp L to cross Cumberland Brook by a waterfall. It is downhill and rocky, running parallel to a wood with rowan and scots pine. Re-ford the stream then meet a road at Clough House. Turn L, ignore a road R to Wildboarclough, and climb up this road shaded by larch, beech and rhododendron until a T-junction. Turn R onto the A54 for 800 metres. Look for the first track L which doubles back uphill. It has a large metal gate, with 'Heild End Farm' and 'No Car Access' signs.

Ride up here curving sharp R then forking L, then round the hill climbing less steeply. The surface is good as is the view of Gradbach Hill ahead. Pass through the next three gates as you descend. At the fourth ignore the track just before it and take the walled lane straight on to a road. Turn L and descend all the way to cross the River Dane and enter Staffordshire. After only about 300 metres take the road sharp R marked Gradbach Youth Hostel and follow it back to your starting point.

Opposite: Alan near Minninglow Grange

23. Minninglow

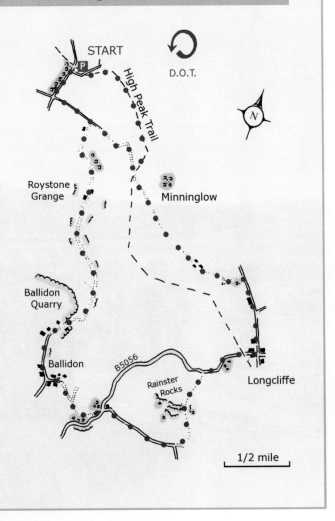

START

D.O.T.

High Peak Trail

N

Roystone Grange

Minninglow

Ballidon Quarry

Ballidon

B5056

Rainster Rocks

Longcliffe

1/2 mile

Route Details

Distance:

8 miles/12.8km

%age off road:

75%

Time:

2 hours

Height Gain:

304m

Map:

OS 1: 25 000 Explorer OL24 White Peak Area

Facilities:

Take a sandwich!

Rail Access:

Cromford station 11km

Route direction

Minninglow car park, Royston Grange, Ballidon, Rainster Rocks, Longcliffe, Minninglow Hill, Roystone

Route Summary

This short limestone route passes through a quiet dry limestone dale where monks had a large sheep farm in the 12th century. Today the sheep are still there but not the monks. A large working limestone quarry, the High Peak Trail (a disused railway line) and a bronze age burial mound all add to the variety of what is basically upland limestone farming country where the soil is thin and any flattish areas are grazed. The trees are rather sparse, ash and hawthorn enjoying such conditions although there are some planted shelter belts. The surfaces are mixed – about half hard track and half grass which can get muddy but almost no road work.

This short but hilly route makes a good evening or morning ride with plenty of trails nearby for those with more time to cycle further, or walk. This route would ride well in reverse too.

Start at Minninglow car park (High Peak Trail) SK194582. Turn R out of the carpark and turn L to head S on Parwich Lane for only 400 metres before turning L again. Ride downhill and take the first track R. This leads down through Roystone Grange in the bottom of an imposing dry limestone dale. You will pass through a farmyard and then pass just L of an old pumphouse.

This pumphouse housed a large water-cooled engine in the 19th century, used to pump compressed air through cast iron pipes (scary stuff!) to drive rock drills in the nearby quarries that had sprung up along the High Peak Trail. It is built on the original site of a 12th century monastic sheep farm which exported wool to Europe.

After a further 800 metres you will emerge in the huge, working Ballidon quarry. Ride straight on through the works taking care to watch out for large lorries and other machinery. Soon after re-joining tarmac, take the first L to climb past Cow Close Farm. Ignore a drive to the L, cross the cattle grid and continue uphill until a sharp L-hand corner. Leave the well-surfaced track here by passing through the large metal gate.

Climb slightly following the old grass track (now with vehicle ruts) before dropping down and round the hill, then zig-zagging to another large gate. Cross the B5056 with care and go straight up the lane opposite. It is 800 metres before this road curves sharp R. At this point turn L through a small bridlegate with the imposing limestone outcrop of Rainster Rocks ahead of you, to the L. The following short section of bridleway is mainly grass so can prove soft going in wet weather. The path heads over to the corner of a wall just R of the rocks. You should follow the L-hand wall to a bridlegate, then cross sides so that you keep the wall to your R.

Climb straight on, past a barn, to the road. Go R, uphill. You will soon pass under the High Peak Trail and should then take the next road L signed 'Aldwark'. After nearly 800 metres you will pass a large farm on your L with lots of lorries. After two more fields on your L, take the wide track L. Negotiate a makeshift gate after only 100 metres and follow the track which soon bears R to a farm. Go through the farmyard and a large gate, then past the snarling (but hopefully, chained) dogs. Ride along the narrow field to and through another large gate. From here basically head straight on! You should first follow the L-hand wall until it curves L, then go straight on until there is a wall on your R. Follow this to the next gateway.

To your R you will see Minninglow, an ancient burial mound topped by a clump of wind-blown beech trees which, along with its height, make it such a distinctive sight from so many places in the Peak District. Here Neolithic tribes constructed 'big stone' chambered tombs to communally bury their dead.

After this gate follow the L-hand wall. Ride straight on through the next three large wooden five-bar gates and down the wide walled lane (which has unfortunately been very badly rutted and cut up by 4x4 vehicles and may be very muddy). This should bring you to the High Peak Trail.

From here are two options:

A. Turn R and follow the trail for 1.5km back to your start point.

B. Go straight across the trail, through the large gate to continue down the walled lane. It descends for 500 metres then curves L. Follow this track uphill (ignoring the tracks R) until you pass a point you should recognise from earlier in your ride and reach the Parwich road. Turn R, then first R again, back to your starting point.

24. Bolsover

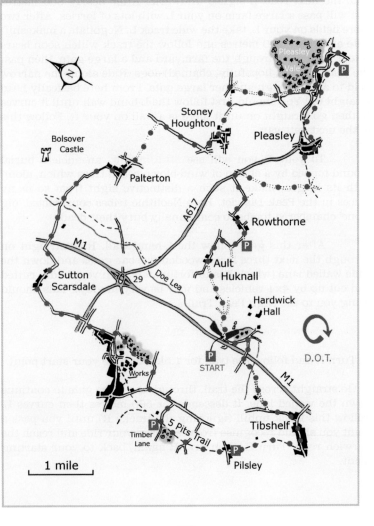

Pleasley
Vale

Stoney
Houghton

Pleasley

Bolsover
Castle

Palterton

A617

Rowthorne

M1

Ault
Huknall

Sutton
Scarsdale

29

Doe Lea

Hardwick
Hall

D.O.T.

Works

START

M1

Tibshelf

Timber
Lane

5 Pits Trail

Pilsley

1 mile

Route Details

Distance:

25 miles/40km

%age off road:

47%

Time:

3 1/2 hours

Height Gain:

310m

Map:

OS 1:25 000 Explorer 269
Chesterfield and Alfreton
*note a small portion of this
route is not covered by this
map.

Facilities:

Pubs and shops on route

Rail Access:

Chesterfield station 10.5km
on small roads if you start the
route at Sutton Scarsdale

Route direction

Hardwick Park, Tibshelf, Five
Pits Trail, Timber Lane, Sutton
Scarsdale, Palterton, Stoney
Houghton, Pleasley, Rowthorne,
Ault Hucknall, Hardwick Park.

Route Summary

Easily accessible from junction
29 of the M1, this route takes
you through the industrial
coalfields of NE Derbyshire.
Cycling on abandoned railway
lines and green lanes, you pass
by old mining villages, opencast
coal sites and reclaimed spoil
heaps as well as large country
houses financed from the
profits of the mining industry.
There is even a choice of 16th
century inn or miners welfare
club for a dinner stop. A rolling
route that is all rideable.

Start at the Hardwick Park National Trust pay and display car park near the great pond SK454637 or nearby in one of the road side laybys. Turn L out of the car park onto the small road and after 500 metres turn R onto Deep Lane. Go over the M1 then after only a few hundred metres take the first track L. Hedged and initially downhill, after crossing a stream it narrows and climbs between two fields of crops. The path soon becomes a track again, passes Biggin Farm and meets a road. Turn L, then next R at the White Hart, heading into Tibshelf.

Continue until you see the Wheatsheaf Pub on your L. Turn L down Station Road just after the pub, and turn L again to head N back under the road on the Five Pits Trail (an old railway line). Follow this undulating trail, crossing two roads until you reach Timber Lane after 3km. Turn R onto tarmac and ride 500 metres up the road to a T-junction where you should turn L. After 600 metres take the second L onto Out Lane signed for Stainsby. Four hundred metres down this road turn L onto the bridleway. Follow this obvious vehicle-width track (initially hedged both sides) for roughly 1.5km to a road. Turn L then first R by the petrol station signed Sutton Scarsdale. At the next T-junction turn R then almost immediately L again signed Sutton.

After 1km in Sutton Scarsdale you should turn R towards Palterton. You will cross the M1 again. As you climb into Palterton curve R staying on the larger road then left up Main Street. Ignore a L to Bolsover. Continue until the next road junction. Here ride straight across onto a hedged track with bridleway fingerpost. This is a great little rural grass track (Palterwell Lane), banked and hedged high on both sides mainly with elder and elm. At the road turn R then after a good 800 metres take the L at a small cross-roads. After 300 metres turn sharp R. As you descend into Stoney Houghton, pass the large farms but look for the first track L (when the road bends sharp R). Go L here onto Water Lane (track), pass the lovely derelict farm with a red tile roof and follow the narrow, winding single path (that may be overgrown with nettles) through woods and ford a stream. The path becomes wider and climbs slightly to a small road. Turn R, not on the road but on the R of the two tracks. It hugs the edge of the electricity sub-station. This wide, bumpier track (Forge Lane) is the 'Archaeological Trail'.

After 1.5km cross the road and take the narrow but hard-surfaced path to Pleasley Vale. You will emerge at the back of a metal engineering works. At the road turn L. Avoid the automatically triggered barriers and ride through Pleasley Vale. You drop off your map here for the next mile or two but come back on, on the disused railway, Meden Trail (northings 65 on map margin). Pass the huge impressive renovated mills.

Continue on this road, past a war memorial. As you climb there is a large sandstone building on your L (Pleasley Vale Nursery). Turn R almost opposite this, pass a metal barrier, under an old height restriction barrier, through the disused car park to a motorcycle barrier and onto the Meden Trail. Follow this disused railway line for roughly 1.5km until a steep descent. Turn L at the bottom. Pass under the A617 adjacent to the River Meden. A very short section of footpath leads to the Chesterfield road. Turn R. Ride uphill past the Nags Head and until you see a roundabout. Turn L just before the roundabout onto Pit Lane.

Follow this until you see a kissing gate on your L. Turn L through the gate and right to follow the old railway line for 800 metres, where you climb onto a banked junction and should turn R. This wide track skirts the edge of the land reclamation work. To your R you will see the old very imposing headstocks and engine houses of Pleasley Pit.

The old Pleasley Pit is notable for a number of reasons. At 2,800ft it was the deepest mine in the East Midlands coalfield and the first deep mine in the area. It was the first mine to use the distinctive steel headstocks and the winding gear was powered by two huge steam engines which although dormant are still more or less intact.

Continue along this track (the lower of two parallel tracks) about 1.5km until you meet a road. Go L, then after 500 metres L again onto Dale Lane. Ride about 700 metres to a T-junction. Turn L here through Rowthorn. Follow the road past Rowthorn Trail. Curve sharp R. Follow the tarmac (ignoring the next L) until a T-junction. Turn L signposted 'Hardwick Hall'. In Ault Hucknall, look for a track L just after passing the graveyard. This takes you to a very impressive blue wooden bridlegate. Go through this into the grounds of Hardwick Hall.

Descend on grass following the crest of the ridge, past a way-mark post then cross the tarmac track at the elbow of its corner. Cross diagonally L over the field towards the bottom L-hand corner and the ponds. At the track turn R, and ride down to the car park where you started.

The engine houses and headstocks of Peasley Pit

View from the high peak trail to Matlock

25. Locko Park

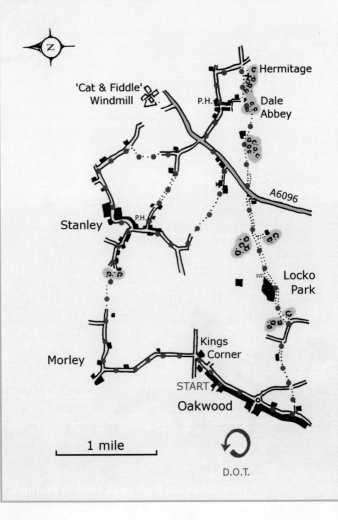

'Cat & Fiddle' Windmill

P.H.

Hermitage

Dale Abbey

A6096

Stanley

P.H.

P.H.

Locko Park

Morley

Kings Corner

START

Oakwood

1 mile

D.O.T.

Route Details

Distance:

12 miles/19.2km

%age off road:

59%

Time:

2 1/2 hours

Height Gain:

130m

Map:

OS 1:25 000 Explorer 259
Derby and Explorer 260
Nottingham

Facilities:

Pubs on route

Rail Access:

Nearest station Derby 5.5km

Route direction

Oakwood, Locko Park,
Dunnshill, Dale Abbey, The
Flourish, Stanley, Hagg Farms,
Stanley, Morley, Oakwood.

Route Summary

This ride, between Derby and
Ilkeston on the edge of the
ever-expanding Oakwood
estate is a real charmer, gently
sauntering through wooded
parkland and hedged green
lanes and across open fields.
Every second building seems
to be a large brick farm with a
handful of stables and horses
to match. It is easy to follow
and isn't hilly. The surfaces are
mixed but generally good and
there are pleasant small woods
with mature oak, lime, beech
and hazel coppices. You will
pass a Hermit's Cave, an old
ruined Abbey and spot the Cat
and Fiddle windmill.

There is a choice of pubs for refreshment. It is an ideal family or evening ride. You will probably meet horse riders; the horses seem very skittish around cycles so slow down and pass wide or stop and let them pass.

Park at Smalley Drive in Oakwood SK 3838. Ride E to Morley Road, turn R, ride down to a roundabout and go straight across. After roughly 600 metres look for a track on your L signposted 'BR No.10 to Locko Park' and 'Morley Road Nos. 136–142'. Turn L up here. It is easy to follow. Cross the first road you meet but at the second turn R. At the next bend take the bridleway L into Locko Park, a metalled drive through park gates. Pass a fruit farm and the large lake on your L. This is a really plush tree-lined parkland drive. Fork next R, still on tarmac, until the surface becomes gravel and there is another split. Go straight on through the gate. The next sandy stretch is a little like riding on the beach!

After the next gate continue straight ahead to cross the road and follow the narrower waymarked path. After a further gate the track becomes wider and gravelly. It soon curves topside of a brick farm, to a gate into a field of cattle. Cross to, but not through the large gateway. Instead follow the top side of the hedge on a path that leads to a large metal gate. Continue on the obvious track through pleasant mixed woodland, through gates as necessary, to reach a smaller gate in front of a house. Turn R through the stable yard and follow the path through Hermits Wood, then across an open field to a road.

At the road turn L, follow it as it curves sharp L and passes the Carpenters Arms pub in Dale Abbey (a prime spot for a little refreshment?). If you want to look around the village it is down to your L. To continue your route, ride along to the A6096 and turn L. After 800 metres take a track R by a bus-stop (signs for 'Hollies Farm' and 'Antiques'). This crosses a cattle grid and leads to another large farm with horse stables. Follow the track between the buildings with the garden of the house to your L.

Curve L following the track which crosses under the electricity lines very close to the large metal pylon. You should find a waymarked bridlegate. Ride the marked track across several open fields to a gravel track and subsequently along to a road.

At the road turn R. Take the next R too, just before the Bridge Inn, marked as a dead end. Follow tarmac along until it falters at Meadow Farm. Ride straight on through the ubiquitous gates to pass an attractive brick farm. At the next buildings (Upper Hagg Farm) turn L (red waymarking arrow and fingerpost), skirting below the brick stables to follow the hedged track downhill. Turn L at the road towards Stanley. Pass through the village but turn R onto Morley Lane just before The White Hart. At the fork go L. You will rise slightly to cross the old (now tree-covered) railway line then turn L on a narrow path between a bench and a small garage (The Midshires Way). This drops to ford a small stream, climbs up a field onto a track, then soon re-joins tarmac where you should continue straight on.

Turn L at the next T-junction onto Lime Lane, then straight on at the crossroads. Turn R after a short distance, back onto Smalley drive where you started.

26. Bakewell & Monyash

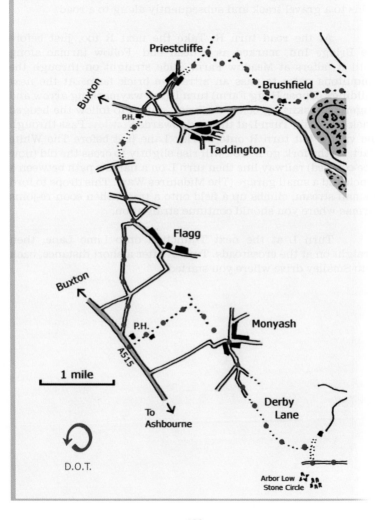

Priestcliffe

Brushfield

Buxton

P.H.

Taddington

Flagg

Buxton

P.H.

Monyash

A515

1 mile

To
Ashbourne

Derby
Lane

D.O.T.

Arbor Low
Stone Circle

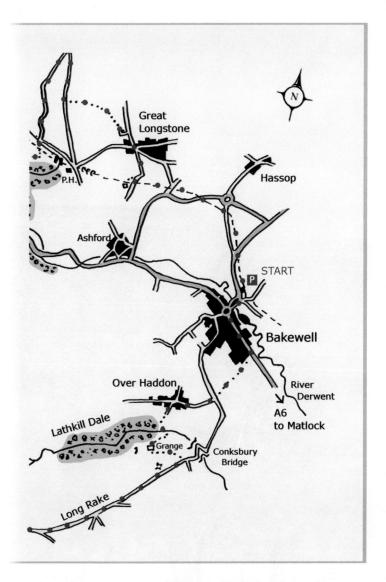

Great
Longstone

Hassop

P.H.

Ashford

START

P

Bakewell

Over Haddon

River
Derwent

A6
to Matlock

Lathkill Dale

Grange

Conksbury
Bridge

Long Rake

N

Route Details

Distance:

26 miles/42km

%age off road:

46%

Time:

4 1/2 hours

Height Gain:

751m

Map:

OS 1:25 000 Explorer
OL24, White Peak

Facilities:

Cafes and pubs at Bakewell,
Monyash, Monsal Head and
Over Haddon

Rail Access:

Nearest station Matlock
13.5km

Route direction

Bakewell,G reat
Longstone,H ayD ale,M onsal,
Brushfield,P riestcliffe,F lagg,
BullI 'th'T horn,M onyash,
DerbyL ane,L ongR ake,
Over Haddon, Bakewell.

Route Summary

This is a hilly and varied day
route, skirting and crossing
limestone dales and farmland
with a real variety of surfaces
and views. Some of the route
is quite high and exposed so it
can be chilly. The majority of
this route is off road and is all
rideable bar a couple of very
short sections.

Start at the old Bakewell Station on the Monsal Trail. There is a pay and display car park here. SK222690. Turn L onto the Monsal Trail, an old railway line, for a flat and easy start. After about 4km you will reach Thornbridge Hall (old station platform) where a small sign points out 'No exit for cycles after this point'. Here leave the trail by going up a step onto the R-hand platform and carry your bike up the flight of steps to the road. Turn L, cycle into Great Longstone to the Crispin pub and go L again.

Take the next R turn signed Longstone Edge, climb up the road for 300 metres before turning L onto a very small tarmac road. Pass Dale Farm, curve R and climb steadily up the walled track on a bumpy but rideable surface towards Longstone Edge. The track bends L then widens and descends gently to a road (Castlegate Lane). Turn R, climb up and over the brow then take the next L at the junction.

Whizz downhill on tarmac (Hay Dale). At the bottom cross both the road and the river, curve L and start climbing. You will pass under the Monsal Trail. At this point it is worth taking a small detour to look at the viaduct by following the trail L for about 600 metres. Return to this spot and climb steeply on the rocky track. Some walking may be needed. After a gate is a flatter section before the track curves R and climbs steeply again. You will follow this track for just over 1.5km to Brushfield. Initially it contours the edge of the top of Monsal Dale with fine views and is walled. It then follows the edge of a couple of fields (unfortunately a bit rutted up by 4x4s) to a large ash tree. Go straight on and downhill soon to reach what was a farm but is now houses. Go through the yard and turn R at the junction with tarmac, uphill signed Priestcliffe and Miller's Dale. Stay on this well-surfaced gated track for the next 2 km to Priestcliffe, ignoring a track right on a sharp L-hand corner near a barn after about 1km.

On re-meeting tarmac at Priestcliffe ride straight on, staying R on the upper of the two small roads. Go straight across the small crossroads and out to the A6 opposite the Waterloo Pub. Cross with care and ride up the walled track, just L of the pub, signed Limestone Way. It is at first rocky and walled both sides as it climbs up the hillside but at the top the surface improves and flattens as you ride along to meet a road. Turn R then L after only 150 metres. At the crossroads go straight on signed 'Flagg', but as the road curves L, turn R onto a small winding road again with a grass 'Mohican' which undulates along for about 1.5km, to a 4-way junction. Don't go L or R but choose the road nearest to straight on and follow it to the A515. Turn L but just after the Bull I'th'Thorn Hotel go L on the track (Hutmoor Butts). You get a good downhill run, past some interesting rare breed farm animals, for just over 1.5km to meet Cross Lane where you should go R out to a road and L into Monyash. The Old Smithy Café is a great spot to have some snap or an ice cream.

From the café and green, take the road S signed 'Newhaven and Youlgreave'. After 400 metres the road curves R but go straight on, on the track/road past the farm, then after 100 metres curve R still on tarmac. There is a gentle climb on tarmac to Summerhill Farm. Tarmac stops here. Ride straight on along the wide, walled track Derby Lane for about 1 km until you reach a large wooden farm gate. If you look L you will be able to make out the head of Lathkill Dale with small limestone outcrops. You will cross the bottom of Lathkill Dale later in the ride.

Go through the large gate onto grass. Follow the L-hand wall of the first field, go through another gateway (muddy) then drop into a grassy dip curving R away from the wall, then L to the gate in the L-hand corner.

Go through this before following the L-hand wall towards power lines. On meeting the farm track from Cales Farm turn R along to the road. Turn L onto the road (Long Rake) and follow it for 3km ignoring all the turns R for Middleton and Youlgreave. You will descend a reasonable distance with views of Over Haddon to the L and Youlgreave to the R.

When you see the first house looming on your L take the track L, one field before the house signed Meadow Place (cattle grid). Follow this to Meadow Place Grange where an impressive courtyard is surrounded by barns. Turn R through the gate between two barns (fingerpost Over Haddon). After the two gates cross the grass field bearing R to another gate and track. This track drops steeply through woods to ford the River Lathkill but then there is a stiff climb to Over Haddon.

As you enter the village, at the first junction curve R, cycle a short way before curving L on Bakewell Road climbing slightly. Curve R then as you leave the village turn R signed Youlgreave. Descend to a T-junction, turn L but after only 100 metres take a bridleway R (Intake Lane). A metal bridlegate leads onto a grass field. Descend following the R-hand edge then onto an obvious track down to the A6. Turn L into Bakewell, go R at the roundabout, cross the River Wye and R onto Station Road. Climb back to your starting point on the Monsal Trail.

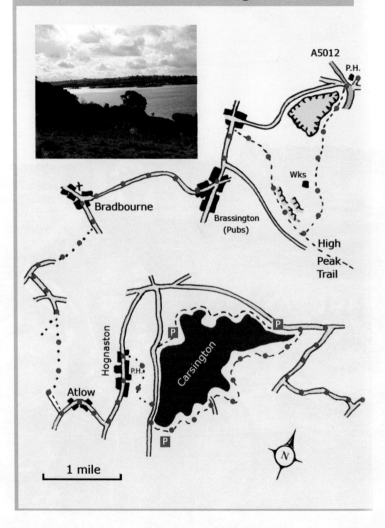

A5012
P.H.

Bradbourne

Brassington
(Pubs)

Wks

High
Peak
Trail

Hognaston

P.H.

Carsington

P

P

Atlow

P

N

1 mile

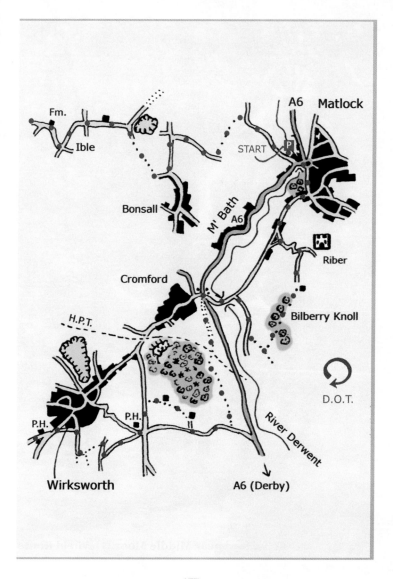

Fm.

Ible

Bonsall

M' Bath

A6

A6 Matlock

START P

Cromford

H.P.T.

Riber

Bilberry Knoll

D.O.T.

P.H.

P.H.

River Derwent

Wirksworth

A6 (Derby)

Ryan at the ford near Middle Moor Hayfield Route

Route Details

Distance:

36 miles/58km

%age off road:

51%

Time:

6-7 hours, a hilly and long day's ride even for the fit rider

Height Gain:

1105m

Map:

OS 1:25 000 Explorer OL24 White Peak Area (small part of route on Explorer 259 Derby, or whole route covered by 1:50 000 Landranger 119 Buxton, Matlock and Dovedale)

Facilities:

Shops, cafes, pubs, tourist information and cycle shop in Matlock, other pubs on route, toilets, cafe, shops and cycle hire at Carsington Reservoir

Rail Access:

Matlock Station

Route direction

Matlock, Riber, Bilberry Knoll, Cromford, Intake Lane, Longway Bank, Gorsey Bank, Callow, Carsington, Hognaston, Atlow Winn, Bradbourne, Brassington, Harboro Rocks, Grange Mill, Ible, Bonsall, Jug Holes, Matlock.

Route Summary

A big day ride for fit riders or split it over several visits. A great introduction to the limestone scenery around Matlock and Carsington. Lots of off-road, short steep climbs and descents. Generally good surfaces, not too much mud. This is a challenging hilly route with a lot of variety. There are woods, quarries, farmland, old railway line and canal, a reservoir and farmland, with both gritstone and limestone landscapes.

In summer especially at weekends the sections around Matlock and Carsington may be very busy. The route involves some road sections as well as lots of tracks with all sorts of surfaces. It is all rideable.

Start at the car park near Matlock railway station SK 295602. From here, walk back to and cross the bridge over the river Derwent. At Crown Square roundabout re-mount and turn R. After 200 metres go straight accross the mini roundabout. You will ride along past the park and football ground then after a pelican crossing you should turn R (signed Starkholmes). Climb uphill past the church and school. The road flattens and passes a small post office. Turn next L onto Riber Road. Climb very steeply ignoring any turn offs until the road flattens and you will see Riber Castle (a Victorian Folly) on your L.

Turn first R onto Hearthstone Lane, follow it along and past the farm. Soon the tarmac peters out. Curve R here onto the sandy/stony walled track. The track climbs to a ridge where it runs along between trees. There is a bumpy section with great views, then a muddy section past beech trees. Keep R at the fork and reach a large gate. Cross down over the next two fields on a rutted track to a large metal gate. After this curve R and follow the track to a tarmac lane where you should turn L. This twisty descent drops you down to the road.

Turn R and follow this road along side and then over the River Derwent, past the imposing Arkwrights Mill (the first factory/birthplace of the Industrial Revolution) to join the A6 (Matlock, Derby road) at a large traffic light junction. Turn L here but R after only 200 metres onto Intake Lane. Climb steeply past housing until the tarmac peters out. Continue straight on, on the tree-lined track into woodland, soon passing under the Sheep Pastures incline. Keep riding uphill to a point where you curve sharp R (a narrower footpath continues straight on) then shortly pass through a metal gate before heading 90 degrees L on a walled track (way-marked Midshires Way).

Follow this well-surfaced, sandy, gated track gently downhill passing a small caravan park before a short rise to meet the B5035. Turn R, cycling uphill for 250 metres then, just after the national speed restriction signs, right onto a tarmac drive/bridleway (sign for Meerbrook Farm). After a few hundred metres curve L, pass through a large gate onto a vehicle-width grass track. This obvious gated bridleway, walled initially, soon crosses a couple of grass fields, before a muddy section, poached by cattle feet, between gorse bushes. Next you join a track where you go L, and follow past Wigwell Nook Farm to the road.

Turn L and ride downhill just over 800 metres to a junction beside the Malt Shovel pub. Turn L then immediately R (signed Breamfield and Alderwasley). After 100 metres turn R onto Breamfield Lane then at the T-junction go R signed Wirksworth, downhill. On the next R-hand corner go L down a farm track without gates. Take it steady on this muddy track as you are quite likely to meet a tractor! When you reach the junction at the bottom turn R, soon back on tarmac and drop steeply into Gorsey Bank. Follow the road across the railway line, along Water Lane out to the B5036 Derby road.

At the Derby Road turn L, keep on the B5023 to cross straight over the mini-roundabout, up a slight rise then downhill, taking the R turn just before the Kingsfield pub (signposted Callow and Kirk Ireton). After 800 metres turn R signed Callow and climb for 1.6km to a T-junction. Go R signed Hopton, uphill initially then steeply down to meet the B5035 where you should head L towards Ashbourne. Pass a R turn to Hopton, then 150 metres on, take the bridleway L.

This circular route around Carsington Reservoir is well surfaced and scenic but has lots of gates and can be busy with families of cyclists and walkers. It winds in and out, up and down following the E side of the reservoir. After 3km you reach a large gate onto a metalled lane, Oldfield Lane. Turn L, cycle uphill about 250 metres, passing the houses on your L then turn R back onto the bridleway way-marked with blue arrows. Follow the way-marking blue arrows until you meet a road just above Millfields car park (toilets/snacks).

Now turn R onto the road. After only 200 metres, pass through the very wide wooden gate (with blue arrows) and ride down the tarmac access track. Tarmac soon becomes gravel. Stay on the gravel surface, splosh through the ford and go through the next large gate. About 500 metres on you cross a stony area where the stream passes under the path before you drop into a dip. Ignore the small footpath gate on your L, climb on up the track for 200 metres then turn L through a large wooden gate into woods. Follow the track beside the stream to the next T-junction. Go L uphill on the track to a road at Hognaston Village.

Turn L and ride downhill crossing the stream then climb for less than 800 metres. Just past a telephone box take a very small road (Furlong Lane) signed Atlow and descend into the village. Turn R by the small triangle of grass, cross a small stone bridge over the stream on a road marked 'unsuitable for motors'. Climb on tarmac until there is a small stone barn on your L. Almost opposite this turn R through the large metal gate next to a step-over stile onto a large grass field. Head uphill riding next to the R-hand hedge. This grassy but rideable climb brings you to a gateway beside corrugated barns. Go straight on uphill on the semi-tarmac track and follow it out to the B5035.

Cross the B5035 (R and immediately L) onto Standlow Lane. At the next junction at the bottom turn R and follow tarmac past New House Organic Farm. Roughly 500 metres on when the road curves gently R towards Banktop Farm you leave tarmac by going through the large metal gate straight on, on a grassy track. Ride down the scenic, gated track to cross Havenhill Dale Brook. At the road turn L and climb into Bradbourne. At the T-junction go R riding for 3km into Brassington. Just past the church on your L take a L turn, then 20 metres on, L again up a steep little road (Jasper's Lane). A short grunt to the brow then descend to a T-junction where you should turn L uphill again 800 metres up the road brings you to Longcliffe crossroads. Turn L signed Ashbourne but after only 150 metres (and before the bridge over the road) go into the old Longcliffe Station through a small squeeze stile next to a gate.

You join the High Peak Trail here and turn L. A fast cinder surface takes you along the flat, past Harboro Rocks. Then cross an access road to Viaton Works. Stay on the trail but after only 200 metres go L through a wooden farm gate (finger post says 'Bridleway to Grangemill.'). Ride up the field edge of the next two fields then on a track for about 100 metres. Fork R back onto grass, through a large gate and down the L-hand side of the field to meet a large surfaced 'works' track. Turn L, fast downhill then up bearing slightly R at a fork. After 1.2km go through the large double metal gate (next to a stile) and along to the next set of gates with a bridleway finger post signed 'Grangemill and Ible'. Go R through the five-barred gate back onto grass.

Race the rabbits on a fun descent. The bridleway is not defined but basically goes diagonally downhill, initially roughly parallel with the electrical wires overhead. You pass through two very muddy gateways and at the bottom pop out opposite the Hollybush pub. Cross the road with care to take the Bakewell road just R of the pub, but after only 75 metres turn R on the small road to Ible. A short way on ignore the R to Ible, climb straight on, following muddy tarmac past a working farm to a cross junction. Go L on a wide track. Initially slightly uphill it curves R then descends to a road. Go straight over onto a bumpier track (Blakemere Lane). After about 1 km you will reach a junction and old quarry entrance. Go R on the track just beside the large metal gate and huge boulder. This follows the edge of a large mud bank hiding the quarry. Soon turn sharp R to follow a muddy walled lane past a couple of farms and back onto tarmac.

At next junction turn L uphill on Abel Lane, down to a T-junction, turn L uphill again (signed 'Bonsall Moor'). After

Above, tree lined gentle riding. Opposite, opening up the taps!
Carsington

less than 800 metres take the first R onto Salters Lane. Another 800 metres of road brings you to a high point. Just over the brow, opposite a quarry track, go L through a metal bridlegate. Here you will get a panoramic view of Matlock, your finishing point! Drop almost straight downhill on a sketchily defined bridleway. Go just beside the small ash tree at the top of the field then as you get further down head for the wall and metal bridlegate in the L-hand corner of the field and below two very large ash trees.

After this gate descend parallel with the L wall to a farm track, curve R and then before the barn go through a large wooden gate on your L. Follow the hedge to join a very muddy track hedged both sides down to the road and turn R. Follow this road back into Matlock, down to the new traffic light juncution near Sainsburys. Turn right here back to the station and your carpark to finish. Well done!!

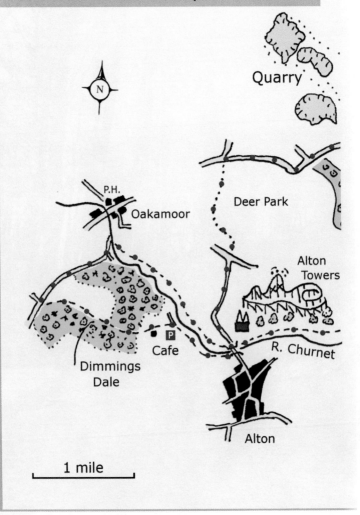

Quarry

Deer Park

P.H.
Oakamoor

Alton
Towers

Dimmings
Dale

Cafe

R. Churnet

Alton

1 mile

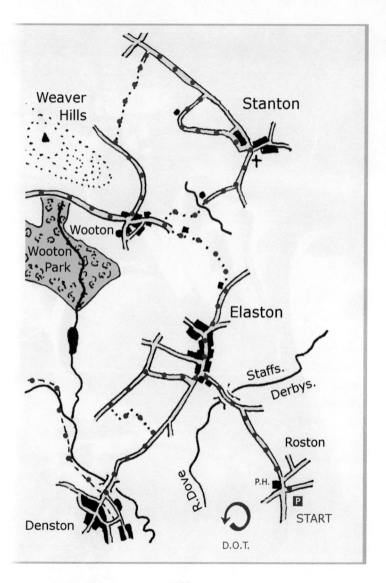

Route Details

Distance:

28 miles/45km

%age off road:

40%

Time:

4 hours

Height Gain:

528m

Map:

OS 1:25 000 Explorer 259
Derby

Facilities:

pubs on route, cafe at
Dimmingsdale.

Rail Access:

Uttoxeter station 14km if you
start the route at Denstone
SK 410099

Route direction

Roston, Ellaston, Michael's
Lane, Wildhay Lane, Stanton,
Wetside Lane, Wootton,
Longshaw, Alton, Oakamoor,
Dimmingsdale, Alton,
Denstone, Lower Ellaston,
Roston.

Route Summary

This ride starts and finishes in
Derbyshire but over 95% of it is
actually in Staffordshire. It is a
lovely wooded route, in summer
very green. In winter it may
be a little dark and muddy on
some stretches. There is some
flat riding and a fair amount of
road work but they are small,
quiet lanes and very scenic.

Start in Roston SK 129410. Parking is only roadside and is limited. Other possibilities may be Roston Inn or Roston Hall. A good alternative start and finish point for this route would be the car park at Dimmingsdale SK 062432. At Roston if parked in front of terraced brick houses turn R in front of Roston Inn onto Mill Lane. An easy, flat, 1.5km along this road takes you to a T-junction where you should turn L onto the B5033. Cross the River Dove into Staffordshire and ride to the next T-junction in Lower Ellastone. Turn R signed Mayfield and Ashbourne, ride 500 metres up through Ellastone, follow the road round a sharp R-hand corner then take the next L signed Stanton.

Ride up this road for only 500 metres, past stone cottages on your L and a large stone farm on your R (Northwood Farm) then go L opposite a fingerpost on a tarmac lane (Michael's Lane). Tarmac soon gives way to a gravel surface at the first cattle-grid. After a house on the R continue straight on, on the gated track, now much more grassy, through one field and then along the edge of another. Rejoin tarmac just after some buildings. Four hundred metres on turn R signposted 'Unsuitable for Motors' (Wildhay Lane). After a cattle-grid follow the obvious gated farm track down to and across a small brook before climbing out to Wildhay and back onto tarmac. After 400 metres turn L uphill to Stanton. You will pass a church then turn L signed 'Cauldon Low and Waterhouses'. Turn next L and after 150 metres go L again onto Chaff Lane. This soon turns into Sladehollow Lane and at a small junction go L. This is a very scenic and tree-lined lane. Follow it for roughly 1.5km round Blake Low.

At the next T-junction turn L. A mile along this road take a track L between the farm house and barns (Wetside Lane). This bumpy vehicle-width track is gated and walled either side and is easy to follow. It becomes a little more grassy and overgrown then runs out at a gate onto a field. Head straight on to follow the left-hand edge of this and the next few fields, soon dropping to meet a small road. Turn L onto this (good panoramic views) and ride downhill into Wooton. Here turn R and then R again onto the road signed Leek. Follow this for about 3km running alongside the ridge of the Weaver Hills. Take the first L signed Cheadle and Oakamoor.

Roughly 1.5km along this road turn L onto Longshore Lane (Bridleway fingerpost). You drop downhill into the deer park. After the cattle-grid and main gate continue to the next gate and cattle-grid. After 100 metres veer off R over grass to a deer-height wide metal gate and through this onto a wooded track. This track can be a little overgrown and muddy but drops to cross a stream. Head L before climbing out to re-meet tarmac. Turn R and at the next road junction follow the signs to Alton (L). The entrance to Alton Towers is on your L so beware of busy traffic. Drop downhill to Alton (roughly 1.6km). As you enter Alton, before crossing the river, turn L just before a large, stone, mill building with planters outside (disused at the moment) and down a track that takes you onto the old railway line.

Turn L, pass under the bridge and past the old station and follow this wooded railway line for roughly 3km until a gate and then at the end of the track a car park near Oakamore. Leave the track here, follow the tarmac road over the metal bridge, then at the small junction turn L (note; there is a picnic site on your R and a pub nearby at Oakamore, again to the R). After your L turn follow alongside the river. After 400 metres ignore the L turn (Red Road) and pedal up the narrow wooded road until the brow of the hill. Descend into a dip where you should take the bridleway L signed Dimmingsdale (just before the house, Old Furnace). Follow this fun, sandy path downhill through woodland. It soon narrows, follows the L-hand side of the stream then mill-ponds. Watch out for walkers, dogs and horses. After a further 1.5km down here, the way-marked bridleway crosses a stream on a small wooden bridge, runs R of one pond then re-crosses the stream and meets a much wider surfaced track.

Turn R. After 300 metres you will reach Dimmingsdale free car park SK 062432 (which would make a good alternative start point) and the Ramblers Retreat, a much appreciated café stop with tea, food and ice-cream and a garden to sit in. From here turn R onto tarmac for just over 800 metres flat riding to a road junction (Alton Bridge Hotel). Turn L, cross Alton Bridge over the River Churnet then take the same track we used earlier by the mill building back onto the old railway line but this time turn R. Follow this for 3.5km to reach the old Denston station platform. The trail stops at a gate. Turn L onto tarmac, L at the next T-junction signed 'Ellastone', then R at the next T-junction, again signed 'Ellastone'. After 1.2km up this B road, turn L onto a vehicle width track (not signposted).

Follow this obvious semi-tarmac track into Prestwood and turn R onto Prestwood Lane (tarmac again). Just 500 metres on turn R at the T-junction then L when you meet the B-road and first R in Lower Ellastone. Cross the River Dove back into Derbyshire. Turn next R onto Mill Lane back to Roston and L when you reach the pub back to your start point.

Aidan on the descent to Blackbrook, Belper Route

29. Belper

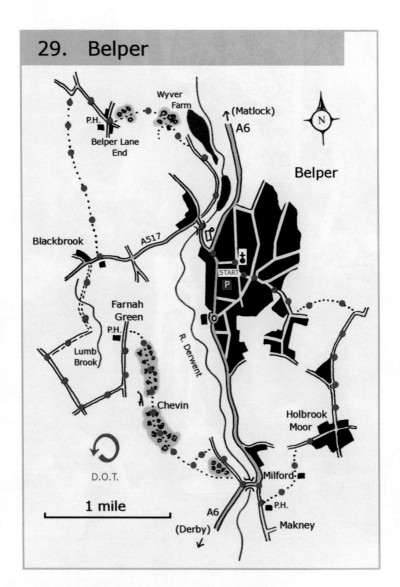

Wyver Farm

↑ (Matlock) A6

Belper

P.H.
Belper Lane End

Blackbrook

A517

START
P

Farnah Green
P.H.

Lumb Brook

R. Derwent

Chevin

Holbrook Moor

D.O.T.

1 mile

Milford

A6
(Derby)

P.H.

Makney

N

Route Details

%age off road:

52%

Time:

2 1/2 hours

Height Gain:

390m

Map:

OS 1:25 000 Explorer 259 Derby

Facilities:

shops, cafes and pubs in Belper, pub at Belper Lane End

Rail Access:

Station in Belper

Route 29. Belper

Route Direction

Belper, Wyver Lane, Blackbrook, Hazelwood, Farnah Green, North Lane, (Chevin), Milford, Dark Lane, Belper.

Route Summary

This medium/short length route around Belper area does not feel in most part at all urban. It follows a number of old lanes, generally with dryish sand and rock surfaces, including the famed Chevin Chase, along through sweet chestnut/mixed woods with fine views. Dark Lane is an interesting sunken lane, and Wyver Farm has the unspoilt feel of somewhere much more remote. The whole area has an interesting history of mills, and many fine buildings remain.There are some high up sections with views of the surrounding countryside, and a few fun rocky sections. It is all rideable.

Start in Belper at the public car park near the railway station (off Field Lane) SK 347475. Turn L out of the car park back to the A6. Turn R onto the A6 towards Cromford. At the large junction and traffic lights turn L, pass the very large brick North Mill and pass over the River Derwent. Then go immediately R signposted 'Wirksworth and Alderwasley' and immediately R again onto Wyver Lane.

Follow this quiet tarmac road for roughly 800 metres. When you see a large gate on your L signed 'Wyver Farm' (opposite a large pond), this is the bridleway you want. Follow this vehicle-width track (with gates) up to and through the yard of Wyver Lane Farm. Ride straight on past the barns (ignore bridleway L) and continue on the obvious track over fields and eventually up to Belper Lane End to re-meet tarmac very near The Bulls Head pub. At the top gate turn R and take the L of the two roads (signed Wirksworth, Shottle and Alderwasley).

At the first farm on the L, turn L into the yard and follow the track bearing R past the sheds to join a narrow single-track that climbs to a junction with a tarmac lane at a sharp bend. Turn immediately L from the single-track then continue straight on. Initially, a tarmac unclassified road this becomes a wide gravelly track. After roughly 500 metres the track curves R towards a farm but you should continue straight on following the slightly sandier track. Soon the path narrows and descends over a tricky but fun rocky section eventually emerging on a drive by Holly House. This drops steeply to the road at Blackbrook.

At Blackbrook turn R then after 150 metres, just after Plains Lane on the R, turn L on the waymarked bridleway by a phone box. Splash through a shallow ford crossing Lumb Brook and climb slightly on tarmac. Follow this vehicle-width track. When tarmac peters out, there is a hard stony surface. After roughly 500 metres you drop to re-cross the brook, before climbing more steeply, on a surface that deteriorates to rutted mud, up to Lumb Grange. On re-meeting tarmac turn R and ride

500 metres along to a T-junction with Over Lane. Turn L and after 750 metres, at the cross junction in Hazelwood, L again. At the next T-junction opposite a large layby turn L. Downhill for 800 metres you will see the Bluebell Pub on your L. Turn R only 75 metres past the pub on a small drive, with bridleway fingerpost. This almost immediately bends sharp R onto a great stretch of sandy, rocky riding (North Lane). Follow it for the next 1.6km and a bit along Chevin Chase, a tree-lined track with good views of Belper to your L. You will start to descend on a rutted, rockier stretch and pass between two halves of a golf course. As you do, start to look for a slight clearing and a narrowish track on the L (not signed). Take this path L to drop more steeply over rocks and roots between trees to a road. Turn R, ride along then down toward the main A6 Derby Road.

Turn L, cross the River Derwent, then go immediately R signed 'Makeney'. After 400 metres. take the first L opposite Makeney Hall onto Hollybush Lane. On the corner is the Hollybush Inn, a good real ale pub. Turn L on the waymarked bridleway Dark Lane (an apt description). It is a slightly sunken track lined by holly and hazel that used to be very overgrown and almost impassable for mud but is now a good hard surface and a pleasant steady climb. Follow this for about 800 metres to a T-junction with Shaw Lane.

Turn R. After 600 metres at the T-junction with the larger Belper Road turn L. Follow it along to a mini roundabout; go straight across (not L) onto Sandbed Lane. When you begin to drop downhill, keep your eyes peeled for the first chevroned sharp corner sign you see, on a R-hand bend. Take the bridleway L immediately before this, which would be easy to miss but once on it, it's an obvious limestone-surfaced double track (it has a footpath fingerpost but is a bridleway).

Follow this track with a grassy centre, past a play area and downhill for about 800 metres to re-meet tarmac at a residential area. At the T-junction turn R and drop steeply into a dip then climb slightly to join a busier road where you should head almost straight on. Follow the town centre signs round a sharp corner but R after only 100 metres onto a small road (Shortlands) that cuts a corner just beside a small car park. Turn L then immediately R onto Church Lane, After 50 metres turn R onto Green Lane then first L onto Field Lane. A short way down here turn L back into your car park start point.

Opposite: the rocky descent to Blackbrook

Quickie Routes

These routes are not short on substance but can be ridden when your time is squeezed. The descriptions are in a different format.

There are no sketch maps or detailed blow by blow instructions. Instead the brief instructions with grid references should be followed on a good OS 1:25 000 map, and visualised or highlighted on your map before you set off. During the ride, the first time you do these routes you will have to use your own map reading skills.

They may not be obvious on the ground. We hope you enjoy them. They cover some new areas and patches not covered by our normal routes.

Harewood Moor Hop

Route Details
Distance:
10 1/2 miles/17km
Map:
OS 1 25 000 Explorer OL24 White Peak

Route direction

Start: lay-by at SK 295673. Take road almost N for 500m then turn R at crossroads. After 1.3km take bridleway R at Harewood Grange Farm. Follow bridleway ESE for 1.4km then L to follow Hungerhill Lane NE for 900 metres to a road. Turn R. After 300 metres take bridleway L. Climb up by Nab Quarry then N to Wellspring Farm and road. Turn R. After 200 metres turn L following the road N. After 900 metres fork R. After a further 0.5km including another R fork reach A619. Cross straight over due N onto track (Westwick Lane). After 300 metres take bridleway L. Follow this NW to pass Bagthorpe Farm. At road and pub SK 318715 turn L. After 400 metres go L onto School Lane. At A619 road turn R then next L. Follow this road 2km to 329m spot height and T-junction at SK 311688. Take bridleway S, 1km to road. Turn R. Follow road 1.5km to a junction. Turn L back to your start.

Beeley Blaster

Route Details
Distance:
10 miles/16km
Map:
OS 1:25 000 Explorer OL24 White Peak

Route direction

Start: Calton Lees car park SK259685. Take the bridleway W about 1.5km to Calton Houses. Next take the bridleway almost S up to woods, then through woods to a 4-way bridleway junction SK 244669. Turn R then L to take the unclassified road beside Aaron Hole Plantation SE to A6. Turn R and follow A6 W for almost 1km then L onto Stantonhall Lane. Follow SW up a very steep hill through Congreave to Pilhough then go L and ride NE downhill to Rowsley. At A6 turn R, cross the river. Turn L on B6012 towards Beeley and R after 200 metres onto Chesterfield Lane. After 600 metres take bridleway N through Rowsley Wood to Fallinge SK

270666 and then NE 1.5km to the road. Turn R uphill. After 0.9km take track L (unclassified road) initially following the top edge of Hell Bank plantation, then downhill W to Beeley Lodge. Turn R onto B6012. Cross the river back to your start.

Fine Strines

Route Details
Distance:
10 1/2 miles/17km
Map:
OS 1:25 000 Explorer OL1 Dark Peak

Route direction

Start: Low Bradfield, near church SK262916. Go N on road to cross Dale Dike then curve W to follow 'Dale Road' for just over 2km. Turn L onto bridleway (Hall Lane) 1.8km back to road. Turn L, follow the road predominately S 2.5km to junction. Turn L then after 100 metres R onto 'Moscar Cross Road' (track) then after 0.5km L to follow track above Moscar Cross Farm. After 700 metres turn L onto 'Stake Hill Road' (track) and follow N for 2km to a road, 'Wet Straw Lane'. Turn L. Take the second road R after 0.5km onto 'Blindside Lane'. Follow along, then downhill 2.2km to Annet Bridge and T-junction. Turn R back to Bradfield.

Win Hill Wander

Route Details
Distance:
11 1/2 miles/19km
Map:
OS 1:25 000 Explorer OL1 Dark Peak Map

Route direction

Start: Heatherdene Car Park SK202860. This route would also work well in reverse. Leave the car park, cross the A6013 and go L to follow the pavement cycleway. After 0.6km go R to cross the dam wall of Ladybower Reservoir. (please walk across the dam wall, do not ride). Turn R to follow the track/bridleway on edge of the woods and side of Ladybower Reservoir. After 1km take the concessionary bridleway (only shown on more recent OS 'Explorer' maps and not signed on ground. It climbs diagonally into woods just beside a footpath fingerpost to 'New Barn') up into Wiseman Hay Clough Plantation. Follow up and round hill for 2km back down to edge of reservoir. Turn L at track junction, follow NW to junction near Hagglee Ford. Turn L steeply uphill on a rocky bridleway to a junction of bridleways at SK159876. Turn L on bridleway (Roman Road) and follow down to Fullwood Stile Farm and down to B-road. Turn L, follow to Hope and the A6187. Turn L, after 1.3km go R onto B6049 towards Bradwell. After 300 metres take road L and then track E to Townfield Lane and through to Wheat Hay Farm SK199823. Turn L to Shatton. At A-road turn L then next R to Thornhill. Go through Thornhill, downhill for 0.5km then L on bridleway/track. Follow to junction. Turn L, then R back across dam wall. Go L on cycle path then R back into car park to finish.

Route Details

Distance:
10 miles/16km

Macclesfield/Cat & Fiddle

Map:
OS 1:25 000 Explorer OL24 White Peak

Route direction

Start: Cat and Fiddle Pub SK001718. This is a very hilly route and although only 16km will probably take well over 2 hours. It is quite high and exposed and can be cold. Not really a Quickie route but a good taste of this area of the Peak District. Take bridleway S then SW past Danebower Hollow for 2km. At A54 turn right SW for 1km then take track R at SK002692 past Sparbent, follow along to then downhill W beside Cumberland Brook to the road. Turn R and follow road to junction SK978714. Here turn L onto the Macclesfield Forest concessionary bridleway for nearly 3km up and down, with a final very steep descent to a road. Go R then L to cross between Ridgegate and Trentabank Reservoirs along to a T-junc. Turn L , pass Bottoms Reservoir then go next R. Follow this road then bridleway along the S side of Tegsnose Reservoir, then up to Clough House. Go right to follow the rough walled track, cross a stream and climb steeply to Hardingland, then even steeper on tarmac heading N for about 0.6km until on a sharp L corner you can go R onto Charity Lane. Follow SE for 1.4km, turn L pass Chapel House Farm and drop down a rocky track to rejoin tarmac. Go L, L again after 100 metres, then stay R and climb on tarmac to the A537. Turn R and follow this busy road back to the Cat and Fiddle.

ACKNOWLEDGEMENTS

Many thanks to Anne and Bob Windsor for hours of typing, proof reading and general help. A big thanks for test riding, photos, company and encouragement to: Ryan Dennis, Lucy Ashworth, Tim O'Neal, David Holden, Sam, Aidan & Jill Lehuep, Alan Leather, John Varley, Keith McKenzie, Gill Denbeigh, Lloyd, Aidan Rumble, Steve Alcock and Ade Martin (in no particular order), & Keir Windsor. Original sketch maps on routes 1-25 by Tim Banton. Original sketch maps on routes 26-29 by Tom Windsor.

All sketch maps and cycle route basemap re-typeset and colour enhanced by Ian Briscoe.

ADDRESSES
Tourist Information
www.visitpeakdistrict.com

Tourist Information Centres:
Peak District Nat. Park Visitor Enq. Line: 01629 816558
Ashbourne (tel) 01335 343666
Bakewell (tel) 01629813227
Bakewell and Castleton Visitor Centre (tel) 01629 816558
Buxton (tel) 01298 25106
Matlock (tel) 01629 583388
Matlock Bath (tel) 01629 55082
Moorlands Centre, Edale (tel) 01433 620207
Upper Derwent Valley (tel) 01433 650953

Access/Rights of Way/ Conservation/Campaign Organisations:
Public Rights of Way Team, Environmental Services,
Derbyshire County Council, Shand House, Dale Rd. South,
Matlock, Derbyshire DE4 3RY / (tel) 01629 585845 / e-mail:
esprow@derbyshire.gov.uk / www.derbyshire.gov.uk/countryside

Derbyshire Wildlife Trust East Mill, Bridge Foot, Belper,
Derbyshire DE56 1XH / (tel) 01773 881188.
www.derbyshirewildlifetrust.org.uk

Chesterfield Cycle Campaign (tel) 01246 555943
www.chesterfieldcc.org.uk
Derby Cycling Group (tel) 01332 451773/345942
www.derbycityccyclinggroup.org.uk

Friends of the Earth, 26-28 Underwood St. London, N1 7JQ tel:
020 7490 1555 / (fax) 020 7490 0881.
e-mail: info@foe.co.uk www.foe.co.uk
Practical conservation tasks,
BTCV Derby, Suite22, Chester Court, Alfreton Rd. Derby
DE21 4AF / (tel) 01332 348591 / www.btcv.org

Public Transport
Traveline – public transport info, for connecting bus services at
the end of train journeys (tel) 0870 608 2608.

Info on public transport: www.derbyshire.gov.uk/buses.
Train times enquiries – National Rail Enquiry Service (tel)
08457 48 49 50 (24hrs every day) / www.nationalrail.co.uk

Cycle Hire Cycle hire centres on the Tissington, High Peak and
Sett Valley trail, in the Derwent Valley and Manifold Valley:
Ashbourne (tel) 01335 343156
Derwent Res. Fairholmes (tel) 01433 651261
Middleton Top (tel) 01629 823204
Parsley Hay (tel) 01298 84493
Waterhouses (tel) 01538 308313 and 01538 308609

National Organisations:
British Waterways – for info. on canal towpaths etc.
E.Midlands Office, The Kiln, Mather Rd. Newark, Notts.
NG241FB / (tel) 01636 704481 / www.britishwaterways.co.uk

YHA Trevelyan House, Dimple Road, Matlock, Derbyshire,
DE4 3YH (tel) 0870 770 8868 / www.yha.org.uk
The National Trust: www.nationaltrust.org.uk
Ordnance Survey: www.OrdnanceSurvey.co.uk

The Countryside Agency, 3rd Floor, Bridgewater House, Whitworth Street, Manchester M1 6LT / (tel) 0161 237 1061

Pennine Bridleway (address above) pbw.info@countryside.gov.uk

Cycling Organisations:
SUSTRANS a civil engineering charity which designs and builds routes for cyclists, walkers and people with disabilities.
35 King St., Bristol, BS1 4DZ / (tel) 0117 929 0888
www.sustrans.org.uk

Byways and Bridleways Trust 01912 364086
Cyclists Touring Club, CTC, Parklands, Railton Road, Guilford, GU2 9JX / (tel) 0870 873 0060 / (fax) 0870 873 0064
cycling@ctc.org.uk / www.ctc.org.uk

The Tandem Club: www.tandem-club.org.uk

Association of Lightweight Campers: www.lighteightcampers.org.uk

TCA Trail Cyclists Association is the national governing body for MTB orienteering: www.trailquest.co.uk

British Cycling – the nationally recognised body for cycle sport in the UK. National Cycling Centre, Manchester, M11 4DQ
(tel) 0870 8712000 / www.britishcycling.org.uk

BCCA British Cyclo-Cross Association (tel) 01325 482052
www.britishcycling.org.uk

Britain's number one mag for bike routes, tests & advice

Available on the first Wednesday of every month.

To subscribe go to www.mbr.co.uk